THE COMPROMISED CHURCH

Copyright © 2020 by Frederick A Herschelman

All rights reserved. No part of this book may be reproduced or used in any manner without written permission of the copyright owner except for the use of quotations or endnotes in a book review.

FIRST EDITION

THE COMPROMISED CHURCH

FREDERICK A. HERSCHELMAN

Introduction

I have had the opportunity to travel, and have visited churches from Fairbanks to Florida, from Hawaii to Maine, and have visited many in between these areas. I have visited many beautiful people, Pastors, and churches. I have met countless talented and dedicated individuals that have contributed greatly towards the Kingdom of God and the Cross of Christ. This book is dedicated to them and all of the strong churches, Pastors, missionaries, and people across America and the Globe. But a pattern was noticed. There were still strong churches that held to traditional Christianity; sometimes they were isolated churches, sometimes they formed a stronghold in their community. But there was another group of churches that were rising up alongside them. They looked the same, acted similar, and used the same terminology, but these churches had new purposes, a new direction, and a new message. Truth was substituted for wealth, the scriptures for self-help, and the cross for the Glory of Man. The heart of the gospel was substituted for the greed of man. This book was written for them.

To what extent will some in the religious system go to hide truth, masquerade their message, and twist their scripture? Why does truth terrify? Why is control used as a substitute for God? Why does non-compliance strike fear, and why is God's church no longer about God in some places? Is the objective of some churches still to glorify God or to create a Theocracy to glorify the leader of the institution or the institution itself? While some Pastors can lie, manipulate, and attempt to twist truth, can they really control truth? Unfortunately this is not an isolated incident. While strong churches, Pastors, and people are still the bedrock of America, new churches are rising up alongside them with new purposes, new agendas, and new directions. They are the Compromised Churches, and they are the greatest threat facing Christianity today.

Table of Contents

I. The Compromise

II. Repackaging Tricks and Selling Them as Truth

III. The Compromised church

IV. Große Übel kamen aus der Kirche

V. Control in the Church

VI. Twisting Truth

VII. History Repeats Itself

VIII. The Study of God

IX. A Quick Tour In Apologetics

X. The Revitalized Church

I. The Compromise

"For the time will come when they will not endure sound doctrine; but after their own lusts shall they heap to themselves teachers, having itching ears; And they shall turn away their ears from the truth, and shall be turned unto fables."[1] That time is upon us now. In many churches across America, The cross of Christ is whored out, on one hand to build legacies and egos, on the other hand for greed and financial gain. Seeking after the heart of God is scoffed at, while felt needs and self-esteem are addressed. The gospel is thrown out so people can "Be a better you" and walk down the line of self-improvement. 2000 years of church history and truth is trampled upon so people's self-esteem and self-interest can be stroked. The original trinity has been replaced by a new trinity: Me, myself, and I. Self-improvement and entertainment guides one arm of the church while wealth creation and greed steers the other arm, and the Bible is used to hand pick verses to justify each movement. In the churches that have not slid into full apostasy, Remnants of gospel ideas can still be found such as love one another or do good things, while the original message is kept hidden. Other groups do not fare as well and have abandoned the almighty, so they can bow their knee to the almighty dollar.

---

[1] 1 Tim. 4:3 (KJV)

2   THE COMPROMISED CHURCH

A facade is put up to keep up the appearance of a church, to keep up income and hold on to the 5013c status, while the heart has moved to greed and corruption. Mansions, jets, and suits are financed, not to help the poor or spread the gospel, but to spread wealth across bank accounts, stock markets, and assets. Some churches now use The Cross of Christ as a bridge for wealth creation and self-interests. Others take the true purpose, and turn it into a new purpose, the creation of legacies, pride, and egos. A movement designed to entertain and distract, soothe and amuse. While these two movements are two separate and different entities, one for self-interests, the other for greed, they are united on one front, and that is the advancement of yourself, rather than that of the Gospel. Welcome to the era of the Compromised Church.

The original gospel message of Christianity has always been under assault by various self-interest groups that promote themselves above Christ, even during the time of the apostles. Various cults, schisms, and false prophets from Christianity have been and are still around today. The difference is that today, these deceivers are permeating mainstream Christianity. The message, for the people who may have gone to church for the last decade and missed it, is that man is a sinner, Jesus Christ died on the cross as a blood atonement for our sins, and with this atonement we have eternal life. "For God so loved the world, that he gave his only begotten Son, that whosoever believeth in him should not perish, but have everlasting life."[2] "If you declare with your mouth, "Jesus is Lord," and believe in your heart that God raised him from the dead, you will be saved."[3] Remaining in your sin and not accepting the blood atonement of Jesus Christ will not lead to life everlasting, but everlasting torment. While many doctrinal differences may have caused strife and arguments, this is the essential doctrine that sent Christ to the Cross, caused Peter to be hung on a cross upside down, Thomas to be speared to death, Paul to be

---

[2] John 3:16 (KJV)
[3] Rom. 10:9 (NIV)

beheaded, John to be exiled, Stephen to be stoned, and scores of other Christians to be sawn in two, fed to lions, or covered in tar and used as torches to light Nero's festivities.

This message has been preached for 2,000 years, it composes church history. Paul composed most of the New Testament with this message. Augustine, Constantine, Billy Sunday, Whitefield, Spurgeon, The Apostles' Creed, The Council of Nicea, and Luther were all unified with the same message. Man is a sinner that has fallen short of the glory of God. The message was preached, and the message worked. Billy Graham led thousands to the gospel through this message. George Whitefield would preach through exhaustion proclaiming the cross of Christ. Luther brought the message to the fallen church. Missionaries across the globe lost lives and saved souls delivering this simple yet profound message.

However, it was decided that this message was not good enough. The message that brought hope to lives would not work in our modern materialistic society. The gospel that stopped the alcoholic from drinking, that brought hope to the hopeless, that changed lives and restored souls, now needed to be kept hidden from people. The opportunity to save someone from the depths of darkness was now something that needed to be locked up. The light that shined was now hidden in a box, and the salt was kept in the salt shakers. People were told a new society needed new techniques, a new era needed a new message. So churches were told that the message of the Cross would not be spoken in church as it might offend new believers. The very message that could bring life and restore souls was kept hidden. The message that traveled from the Middle East, to Rome, to the Americas, to across the globe, is now a secret message, a message that is hidden below convenience.

So the idea for the Seeker Sensitive church was created. The original idea behind this was to bring many new believers or seekers to the church and not present the gospel message or the idea of sin during

Sunday mornings as it could offend people, but reserve that for Wednesday nights and the more serious believers. This way new seekers could be introduced into a friendly atmosphere and not be offended by the Cross of Christ. After finding the friendly atmosphere inviting, these seekers would be ushered into Wednesday night classes that would offer more substance and value. This was a logical approach backed by savvy marketing material that made sense and seemed worth a shot. Unfortunately, in many churches, the in-depth Wednesday night programs quickly dissipated. It was a classic bait and switch.

Robert Schuller was one big influence in the reintroduction of this movement; he would ask people in the neighborhood what they wanted out of the church. The objective here was not to scour the scriptures to teach the people how to live in righteousness to please God, but to see what kind of atmosphere the unsaved people would like and deliver that. Kind of the idea behind how some children may be more excited to spend a weekend with the Grandparents who give them ice cream and candy, rather than their parents who may discipline them and make them eat vegetables. Give the people what they want, rather than what is good for them. But Robert Schuller would not work for mainstream Christianity, so a large church out of Chicago became the face of the movement. This church accomplished great things that the secular and Christian world looked up to.

And a lot of good did manage to come out of the church. This church grew in prominence, and the lead Pastor became a Pastor that other Pastors sought after. Many charities were created, and large volumes joined the church. The church became a replica that other churches would follow. So you had churches making a copy of a copy. Over time, churches departed from having anything to do with the original gospel message, the original purpose of church, and started creating institutions unto themselves. Church then became about how beautiful the building was, how great the pastor was, how dynamic the programs were, and how much better this church was compared to the rival church. Legacies, Pride, and Egos were created and established. Big buildings sprouted from the ground and campuses were built, excitement and enthusiasm pushed grand dreams, big budgets, and vivacious visions. People were on the move, and big things were going to be accomplished that future generations would read about. In the excitement and business of everything, the gospel message, the original point of church, was left behind.

The man that some consider the founder of the movement encountered allegations of misusing his position of authority to sexually harass and have affairs with his co workers.[4] The allegations were denied, and the elder board paid for its own "investigation" into the matter and found the pastor clean. The entire Elder board stood by the Pastor. However, more allegations and women were then discovered.[5] Prominent people, authors, and members did the right thing and stood up for truth. The entire elder board then resigned. The next lead pastor in line then resigned. The other lead pastor in line also then resigned. Later on, it was discovered that the co-founder of the church was accused of clergy sexual abuse.[6] While this church very well might have fed multitudes and done numerous charity programs, their own compromises that they established shook the foundations of the church. On one hand you have a person who was put in a superstar position and made a mistake. On the other hand, you have to question why you would continue to follow a

---

[4] Goodstein, Laurie. "He's a Superstar Pastor. She Worked for Him and Says He Groped Her Repeatedly." The New York Times. The New York Times, August 5, 2018.
https://www.nytimes.com/2018/08/05/us/bill-hybels-willow-creek-pat-baranowski.html.

[5] Jones, Emily. "Traumatized Willow Creek Megachurch Turns Corner, Asks Ex-Pastor Bill Hybels to 'Repent' of Sexual Misconduct." CBN News, August 1, 2019.
https://www1.cbn.com/cbnnews/us/2019/july/traumatized-willow-creek-megachurch-turns-corner-asks-ex-pastor-bill-hybels-to-repent-of-sexual-misconduct.

[6] Miller, Emily McFarlan. "Willow Creek Confirms Abuse Allegations Against Gilbert Bilezikian." News & Reporting. Christianity Today, January 28, 2020.
https://www.christianitytoday.com/news/2020/january/gilbert-bilezikian-dr-b-abuse-confirmed-willow-creek.html.

movement founded on deception and corruption, whose roots are stained, rather than follow the leader of another movement, who was sinless.

Unfortunately this is not an isolated incident and has become a prevalent theme among many modern-day churches, both large and small. The lead pastor, generally a charismatic, intelligent man with obvious great public speaking abilities, aligns himself with elders who are supposed to provide moral accountability, but in reality are glorified yes men and puppets. Elders are not picked to be beacons of righteousness, but are picked to be molded and manipulated, to agree to the Pastor's policies, and to give the appearance of accountability. Pastors are then able to use the pulpit for wealth enrichment and glory, instead of the gospel. Fear, control, intimidation, and manipulation secure their dominion over their Theocracy. Absolute power corrupts absolutely.

To give credit where credit is due, this church did issue an acknowledgement of sorts, citing some of the weaknesses in the seeker movement and attempted to make a change. They acknowledged: "We made a mistake. What we should have done when people crossed the line of faith and become Christians, we should have started telling people and teaching people that they have to take responsibility to become 'self feeders.'"[7] They even completed their own Reveal surveys and published their own Reveal Study which showed that some of the principles that the seeker church was founded upon did not work and acknowledged that members wanted a deeper relationship focused on scripture. They discovered that "Many were considering leaving. And some of our most mature and fired-up Christians wanted to go deeper in their faith and be challenged more but felt as if our church wasn't helping them get to the

---

[7] Burney, Bob. "A Shocking 'Confession' from Willow Creek Community Church." Christian Headlines. www.christianheadlines.com/news/a-shocking-confession-from-willow-creek-community-church-11558438.html (accessed Feb. 6, 2020).

next level."⁸ They did acknowledge that: "Those who are growing in Christ don't want us to beat around the bush. They expect that we will teach them the Bible, challenge them to examine their lives, and encourage them to make whatever changes are necessary to conform to the truth they are hearing."⁹

Unfortunately what happened here may have opened the door to deception, but what is going on in today's churches no longer has anything to do with this church. Churches started copying and making copies of a copy, but are now heading in their own direction with their own purpose. After you submit to the great compromise, substituting the gospel message for numbers, you are susceptible to all of the minor compromises. Without a source of truth, a standard of righteousness, a concrete foundation, it is a slippery slope on the way to Apostasy. Everything goes in the new Wild West arena of morality. Pastors across America contradict themselves on how they interpret the Bible. The moral standard of today will be changed by tomorrow, as the standard is defined by cultural acceptability and not the Bible. Instead of looking at the Bible as a source of inspiration to fight against the culture, the culture is examined to see how the Bible can align with it.

People come to church for a variety of reasons. Maybe it is to maintain their social status in the religious community. Maybe out of curiosity. Maybe eager to hear a message that could revive their faith. Maybe out of family tradition or to feel better about themselves. Some, at some churches across America come to find an answer, to fill the empty void in their hearts, to see if there is an answer to the emptiness found in their lives. Some have tried the world's system, the world's methods, and played by the world's rules and found that something was still missing; they came up empty. Many men chased wealth and came up empty. Many

---

[8] Hawkins, Greg L., and Cally Parkinson. *Move: What 1,000 Churches Reveal about Spiritual Growth*. Grand Rapids, MI: Zondervan, 2011., p. 9.
[9] Ibid., 54.

have chased pleasure and found despair. Many have sought fame and found loneliness.

The book of Ecclesiastes details a man named Solomon who ruled Israel during its time of greatest wealth and economic prosperity. The man had access to wisdom, wealth, riches, pleasure, women, and power, in vast abundances that most people will never experience. Over time he found the experience of having access to unlimited wealth, power, and women, to be futile, pointless, and weary. He concluded with: "Fear God and keep his commandments."[10] The emptiness that Solomon found in Ecclesiastes is found today. Americans have a tendency to constantly place a goal in front of them, if this milestone is achieved peace will be found, if this milestone is reached, happiness will be found, if this goal can be accomplished, our family will be restored. New goals are continually created and chased, as the previous goal is rendered futile, the new one must hold the answer. But they do not. It is when all of the world's voids are filled, that the emptiness can remain the deepest. Most people strive and never reach, but sometimes when you do reach and get what you spent your life striving for, the emptiness can feel the deepest. This is what has caused movie stars to end their lives. While many may not have experienced the depths of sorrow and emptiness and meaningless found in Solomon or a Hollywood movie star, remnants of that emptiness are found in hearts across America. And that emptiness is found in Churches across America. So every Sunday, people try the church, try to find a solution. But in many of today's churches, answers are not found. Plays, entertainment, fellowship, or "love" may be found, but the truth is kept hidden. What can save a soul or change a life is kept out of the grasp of those who need it most. You can't go to a restaurant and not get food, you can't swim in a pool without water, you don't go to a golf course to not play golf, but apparently you can go to a church and not get the gospel.

---

[10] Eccles. 12:13b (KJV)

Compromise, deception, and apostasy within God's people is generally not a new idea; it has been around since before Christ. Daniel was tossed in the lions' den because while all of his peers would bow to the Babylonian idols, he refused. Jeremiah, the weeping prophet, had to foretell the destruction and captivity of Judah by the Babylonians. Isaiah reminded the people that they needed to keep God's covenant if they were going to remain God's chosen people. Hosea, Joel, Amos, Obadiah, Zechariah, Jonah, Haggai, Zephania, Nahum, Micah, Habakkuk, and Malachai, all warned God's people to turn from false idols and the compromises of the day. King David fought with his weapons of war. But before becoming king, he had to work around the previous king, a powerfully built man who had God's favor and anointing as his chosen leader, but lost favour with God because he turned away from God and relied on witchcraft, rather than the Creator. Today the enemy is picking off previous men of God across America, one by one. They can stand on their legacies, they can tout past accomplishments when they did walk with God, but they currently are just around to lead people down the path of destruction, just like they are headed.

This is not just limited to the Old Testament. Jesus Christ and the apostles spent a majority of their time dealing with false teachers of the day and warning about false teachers to come. Warnings about deception and false teaching is weaved through the fabric of the Bible. The culture of the day was violent and debauchery was the standard. Suetonius tells us of wild exploits from all of the Emperors. Nero, who martyred Paul and numerous others, had sexual relations with his mother and sister before allegedly killing them. He castrated little boys to go on swims with him prior to his evening entertainment of running people over in his chariot at night. The culture and morality of the day flowed over to parts of the church at that time. Paul has to deal with the carnality of the Corinth church which mimicked the culture and was steeped in sexual immorality when he states: "It is reported commonly that there is fornication among you, and such forniction as is not so much as named among the Gentiles, that one should have his father's wife."[11]

Humans sin, and the struggle against sin is a constant lifelong battle. The heart of the gospel is that the blood of Jesus can wash these sins from your life and you can have a fresh start. It is the redemptive process that true Christians need. It is not a coincidence that all of the biblical prophets had repentance as their major theme, it is the practice that the Christ follower needs to walk on the path of Christ. The Lord's Prayer has repentance built into it. Running sprints may not be fun, but if you are on the track team, you are going to need to do this. Football players may not enjoy two-a-day practices, but they may be necessary to form a championship team. Going to college can be a financial and academically challenging endeavor for some, but it may be necessary for those whose career needs that particular education. In the same way, you can't continue a walk with Christ through leadership seminars or glorified self-help groups, but refining yourself through prayer, the forgiveness of sins and repentance, and reading the Bible. These are the attributes the Compromised Church strikes to cease while maintaining their religious structure. "Having a form of godliness, but denying the power thereof: from such turn away.[12]" The problem is when you remove the idea of sin and judgment, all you are left with is entertainment and self-help. It doesn't take long to figure out that the church is not going to add any value to their lives outside of a great social club or a welcome diversion to the busy week. It perpetuates this idea that if you pop into the building for a hour a week, socialize with like-minded people, and throw in part of your paycheck, the problems of this world are going to melt away and your family will be restored. Adding to the problem instead of resolving the problem.

---

[11] 1 Cor. 5:1 (KJV)
[12] 2 Tim. 3:5 (KJV)

The Attractional church / Entertainment model brings exciting elements into the church such as digitally enhanced presentations, entertainment, powerful speakers, nice buildings, some even with mini amusement parks inside them. And there is nothing wrong with an attractional church model if it is done correctly. There is a church in Michigan that is putting out Biblically based movies and another church in Florida that has a large outdoor kids playground that attracts the community. Some churches show a quick video clip followed by a strong Biblically infused sermon. This is all great. Beautiful, welcoming, digitally enhanced power house churches proclaiming the truth are a nice, modern day way to reach people. But you have to have the message, you have to have the truth, you have to keep the central point of it. Without the gospel, without the message, you have missed the point. And the attractional church needs to be used to present the gospel, not create an attractional church to create numbers. By the time you have Van Halen on stage performing worship, open up a brothel, and have beer kegs on tap, you have missed the point. Or if you just have a nice attractional church that draws in crowds but has no message, no substance, no truth, you likewise have missed the point.

In many churches across America, we are seeing a new agenda and a new direction. Today we have numerous church movements infiltrating into the churches. We have the emergent or emerging church that is emerging from traditional Christianity to give us a diluted gospel and to focus on some of the good aspects of Christianity like helping the poor, loving neighbors, and building strong communities while neglecting the gospel message. "There be some that trouble you, and would pervert the gospel of Christ. But though we, or an angel from heaven, preach any other gospel unto you than that which we have preached unto you, let him be accursed. As we said before, so say I now again, If any man preach any other gospel unto you than that ye have received, let him be accursed."[13] Then we have the entertainment driven / attractional church where each and every service tries to outdo the previous one and make sure that the audience is entertained throughout with jokes and stories. "Many U.S. churches today have 'forgotten' their purpose, becoming entertainment-driven social organizations eager to blend in with secular culture instead of focusing on biblical discipleship."[14] The objective is to puff up entertainment to draw in the crowds, but according to Dr. David Jeremiah: "In many respects, young people are demanding more truth, more teaching, and less entertainment. They're not interested in shallow expressions of religion."[15]

We have the prosperity gospel, which takes some truths of scripture and twists them to destroy the sheep, some going as far as to say Christ did not die on the cross for the salvation of your sin, but for your financial gain. We have the universalism movement which looks to blend the salvation message across all people and all religions to present the idea that all paths lead to salvation. This contradicts numerous biblical references, such as John 14:6 "I am the way, the truth, and the life: no man cometh unto the Father, but by me."[16] We have the New Age Movement, which is heavily infiltrating many churches. Books are written by former New Age members that have left the movement and are surprised to see numerous New Age ideas and principles in the church. Legalists have always been a problem, but if righteousness was attainable through the law, Christ would not have needed to die on the cross. The opposite of the legalists, are the churches that are supporting a sort of hyper-grace. An anything goes mentality to sin. But we need to repent and live under the Lordship of Christ. "For the wages of sin is death; but the gift of God is

---

[13] Gal. 1:7b-9. (KJV).
[14] Jeremiah, David. "David Jeremiah warns modern church is entertainment-driven social organization afraid of controversy." The Christian Post. www.christianpost.com/books/david-jeremiah-warns-modern-church-is-entertainment-driven-social-organization-afraid-of-controversy.html (accessed Feb. 6, 2020).
[15] Ibid.
[16] John 14:6 (KJV)

eternal life through Jesus Christ our Lord."[17] Together, pieces and aspects of all of these movements have given us the Compromised Church, and it is the greatest danger facing Christianity today.

---

[17] Rom. 6:23 (KJV)

II. Repackaging Tricks and Selling Them as Truth

In 1517, Dr. Martin Luther posted his 95 theses on the doors of the Wittenberg Chapel. His paper transformed lives and revolutionized the church. Blood was shed, wars would be fought, and people were burned at the stake. The church was torn in two, sides were taken, lives were spent, Luther himself was surprised his flesh was not the first to be burned, and was disappointed, as he was worried that God did not consider him worthy to be martyred for the gospel. Luther wasn't trying to split the church or change the course of world history, he simply wanted answers to his questions, answers the church wasn't able to provide.

Years later, a man named Michael King took a trip to Germany, and was so inspired by Martin Luther that he legally changed his name from Michael King to Martin Luther King. His son was a junior, so he changed his name also. As the original Luther risked his life to free his people from bondage and oppression, so did this man's son, until an assassin's bullet took the life of Dr. Martin Luther King Jr. on April 4, 1968.[18]

Today we have many denominations that broke off from the Catholic Church, during the Protestant reformation initiated by Luther. But what did he do that was so significant that he changed the course of World History? What beliefs did he consider so compelling that he

---

[18]Metaxas, Eric. *Martin Luther: The Man Who Rediscovered God and Changed the World*. New York: Penguin Books, 2018, **1.**

refused to recant them at the Diet of Worms in 1521, risking his life? Was this just a preference for a different worship style? Minor doctrinal difference? Some Theological differences? Different Eschalatogical views? Sprinkling vs. immersion? What was all the uproar about?

Europe in the 16th century was different politically, socially, structurally, and economically from modern 21st century America. There were peasants and kings, knights, & serfs. There were castles and plays, orchards and vineyards, and Gutenberg had a new thing out called the printing press, but there were no vehicles, television, or internet. Christopher Columbus had recently sailed the ocean blue from Spain to America. The Eastern wing of the Roman Empire, officially known as the Byzantine empire, finally collapsed after the Ottoman Turks sacked Constantinople. The Middle Ages were coming to a close which brought various plagues along with numerous wars and famines, and Europe was entering a new era called the Renaissance. It was an exciting period which brought new ideas in philosophy, literature, and art. Michelangelo completed his masterpiece of David on the ceiling of the Sistine Chapel. Leonardo Da Vinci completed his Mona Lisa. Copernicus writes Commentariolus, stating the sun is the center of the universe. Machiavelli writes *The Prince*. And then a German monk started writing, and these words would shake the rest of the empire and the known world. The Reformation would now be launched.

Out of the many historical differences that were present in 1517 when Luther composed his 95 Theses, one of the largest differences was the church. People did not have options whether they wanted to attend a Lutheran church, Baptist Church, Non-Denominational Church, or Pentecostal Church, as all of these denominations would be branched off from the Protestant Reformation, which Luther's writings launched. There was the Catholic Church and that was it. The Catholic Church was all powerful, it controlled everything, including and most importantly your eternal salvation. The Catholic Empire at this time controlled one third of the land in Europe. The Priests were responsible to baptize, help with confessions, administer last rites, and various social service programs. They read the Bible for the people and told them what the Bible says, as the Bible was in Latin and most people in that area read German. The Pope held the authority over all of the kings in Europe, as they had to bow to him as his power came from the Roman Empire. The Catholic Church had the authority to tax you, kill you, torture you, or take your land. You were forced to pay tithes to the Catholic Church and then pay fees on top of your tithes. If you spoke up against the Church, you could be excommunicated, which would mean that you would be exiled from all Catholic Church functions. It also meant you would be left without a path to eternity, according to the Church. Unless they decided to just kill you, which was always a possibility. The Catholic Church controlled everything politically, socially, and religiously. It was all powerful. The church took the place of God, you could pray to the church's icons, and salvation was found in the church's pay to play system for salvation. When Luther was excommunicated from the church, they weren't saying he could no longer attend the local potlucks and barbeques, they were saying he was eternally damned to hell in the future, and for now, a good burning at the stake should suffice.

On top of the tithes, the church would collect money from relics and pilgrimages. The wealth of the Roman Catholic Church was unprecedented; they controlled as much and had as much wealth as some of the great empires of World History. But when greed comes into play and the question of how much is enough is asked, the answer is always more. Everything was for sale, positions in the church were bought, peasants had to pay for a child to be baptized, and peasants paid for each service, on top of their tithes and working the church land. On top of these other fees, the Catholic Church created a system called indulgences. Indulgences were certificates that you could purchase to cover past and current sins. If you just purchased these indulgences, then you were covered. They had all kinds of indulgences and point systems to cover your sins and guarantee your salvation. You even had an obligation to purchase indulgences for dead family members and relatives, so they could get out of purgatory, in case they were not able to purchase enough indulgences during their time on this earth. Indulgences could even be purchased for future sins that were about to be committed. In one interesting scenario, a man purchased indulgences to cover his future sin of robbing the man that was selling indulgences.[19]

It was these indulgences that Luther started speaking about. He necessarily did not want to take on the Herculean task of taking on the Catholic Empire by himself, he just couldn't stand to see these poor peasants giving what little they had to try to purchase their salvation from the church. Luther's attacks started with indulgences then moved to the Reformation Solas. Sola Scriptura, Scripture alone. Sola fide, Faith alone, Sola gratia Grace alone, Solus Christus, Christ alone, Soli Deo gloria, To the glory of God alone. Luther saw salvation through faith. Luther said the Church's rituals did not help and that the church was not infallible and actually made many mistakes, actually all of the time. People did not need to turn to the Church, but to turn to God. What started with indulgences, ended with revolution. People's faith was questioned, long-held beliefs were examined, wars would be fought, and the powerful Catholic Empire was brought to her knees and torn in two by a humble monk with a pen. While Luther originally tiptoed around the power of the pope, he later boldly proclaimed that the Pope was an AntiChrist sent by the Devil. While Luther was excommunicated from the church and died with a bounty on his head under a proclamation that anyone could kill him on

---

[19] Metaxas, Eric. *Martin Luther: The Man Who Rediscovered God and Changed the World*. New York: Penguin Books, 2018, **106.**

sight, his actions freed millions from the bondages of religion and changed the course of World History.

Today the Catholic Church no longer exerts the authority it once had. In its place a new gospel and a new system has risen. Today indulgences are not purchased, people are not killed, salvation is not listed for sale. This time around, you are not purchasing for eternity, but purchasing for "favor" and "anointing," for right now. It is called the prosperity gospel, and old ideas have been repackaged into new methodologies to gain wealth for a few, again, at the expense of the sheep. In Luther's day, religious figures would tell you that you needed to pay money to atone for your sins to keep your salvation. Today, you are told that you need to pay money to have God's favor and anointing in this life. As this life takes precedence over eternal life, a lack of giving and faith is always the response to the lack of money or healing. Under true prosperity theology, if you speak against these "Men of God," you will be cursed and lose God's blessing. But if you give enough money to support their greed, you will be healthy, wealthy, and prosperous. The money can not go towards frivolous tasks such as spreading the gospel, helping the poor, and feeding orphans, but for yachts, jets, and mansions. "But though we, or an angel from heaven, preach any other gospel unto you than that which we have preached unto you, let him be accursed. As we said before, so say I now again, If any man preach any other gospel unto you than that ye have received, let him be accursed." [20]

The prosperity gospel guarantees a happy, healthy life to those who adhere to it. It started with the Word of Faith movement, originating from E.W. Kenyon, championed by Kennith Hagin, expanded by Oral Roberts who was able to add the seed-faith concept, and then fully monetized by Kenneth Copeland. Dutifully following the correct leaders, faith, positive speech, and donations leads to your lottery ticket on earth and

---

[20] Gal. 1:8 (KJV)

guaranteed good health and wealth. Positive proclamations are the root of the Word of Faith movement. It starts off with proclaiming victory verses for your life. And this can start off as a good thing as memorizing and speaking verses in your mind over and over again is good and many people have received victory over stress, fear, and anxiety from this. Saying and proclaiming positive things and verses is a great thing. A top-level champion athlete never enters a contest thinking he does not have what it takes to win. Likewise, hanging around a negative person consistently and listening to the negative talk does wear you down and destroy you over time. If you constantly tell your children they are no good or are abusive towards them, they will never flourish to their true potential. Likewise, if you speak encouraging words to them and constantly uplift, encourage, and motivate, they will flourish. The problem is, like the other cults or unhealthy churches, they take a good thing and then twist it. Some in The Word of Faith movement have taken good things and twisted and tortured them to destruction. Verses are used to try to bend the will of God so that its adherents can even become their own "Little gods." Advanced disciples of the doctrine don't even have to pray to God, you can just pray to yourself. Saying and proclaiming the right set of words and eliminating negative thoughts will guarantee health, wealth, and success. Advanced disciples of the movement learn that they need to cut the negative people out of their lives that "Drain" the energy from them. It starts with friends and ends with family members. The problem is, while positive proclamations may work in some scenarios in limited avenues, you can not positively proclaim yourself into heaven.

In prosperity circles, all of the sermons, time, and energy is devoted to increasing your favor and status with God to increase money for yourself. Not through indulgences and for eternal salvation, but for favor right now by purchasing it through the prosperity preacher. They are able to justify their greed and that of some of the congregants by saying that in return, you might bless someone else or do good with it. They will spend their lives pursuing money and wealth and in return, they may, on occasion, if time permits, give a token amount away if it can be documented. "For The love of money is the root of all evil: which while some coveted after, they have erred from the faith, and pierced themselves through with many sorrows. But thou, O man of God, flee these things; and follow after righteousness, godliness, faith, love, patience, meekness."[21] What embodies the love of money more than spending all of your preaching time talking about it, all your free time thinking about it, and all your active time working towards it? "Perverse disputings of men of corrupt minds, and destitute of the truth, supposing that gain is godliness: from such withdraw thyself.[22]

The problem is that the prosperity gospel does not match up to the Bible, logic, or common sense. If Godliness was always directly tied to financial prosperity, Jeff Bezos, Bill Gates, and Warren Buffett are our current leaders. Godly men of past history include Pol Pot, Idi Amin, Ivan the Terrible, Stalin, and Hitler. According to the *Foxe's Book of Martyrs*, John may have been able to live the island life, but the rest of the disciples were beaten, crucified, beheaded, speared, or stoned. John Piper stated: "If God's love for his children is to be measured by our health, wealth, and comfort in this life, then God hated the Apostle Paul." When Jesus was fasting for 40 days, "Again, the devil took him to a very high mountain and showed him all the kingdoms of the world and their glory. And he said to him, "All these I will give you, if you will fall down and worship me."[23]

> The implications and problems of the prosperity gospel are that it takes a gospel designed to help others and save the world and puts the focus on ourselves. It undermines attempts to relieve poverty, puts the burden of blame on the poor and sick instead of helping them, discredits the

---

[21] 1 Tim. 6:10-11 (KJV)
[22] 1 Tim. 6:5 (KJV)
[23] Matt. 4:8-9 (ESV)

relationship between work and wealth, distorts basic economic principles, and the heart of the prosperity gospel, greed, prevents true contentment.[24]

The problem is not if God answers prayers. He does: "If you had faith like a grain of mustard seed, you could say to this mulberry tree, 'Be uprooted and planted in the sea,' and it would obey you."[25] The problem is not that faith isn't good, because it is: "Blessed is the man that trusteth in the Lord, and whose hope the Lord is. For he shall be as a tree planted by the waters, and that spreadeth out her roots by the river, and shall not see when heat cometh, but her leaf shall be green: and shall not be careful in the year of drought, neither shall cease from yielding fruit."[26] The problem isn't that faith can be rewarded: "This book of the law shall not depart out of thy mouth; but thou shalt meditate therein day and night, that thou mayest observe to do according to all that is written therein: for then thou shalt make thy way prosperous, and then thou shalt have good success."[27] The problem isn't that God can reward us now: "Blessed is he that considereth the poor: the Lord will deliver him in time of trouble. The Lord will preserve him, and keep him alive; and he shall be blessed upon the earth: and thou wilt not deliver him unto the will of his enemies."[28] The problem isn't if God can heal, because God heals: "And the prayer of faith shall save the sick, and the Lord shall raise him up; and if he have committed sins, they shall be forgiven him."[29] The problem isn't that positive declarations don't work, because they do: "Death and life are in the power of the tongue: and they that love it shall eat the fruit thereof."[30] The problem is the manipulation of these items and the manipulation of

---

[24] Dr. Andrew Spencer, *"The Importance of Rejecting the Prosperity Gospel"* Institute for Faith Work and Economics, January 28, 2014.
[25] Luke 17:6 (ESV)
[26] Jer. 17:7-8 (KJV)
[27] Josh. 1:8 (KJV)
[28] Ps. 41:1-2 (KJV)
[29] James 5:15 (KJV)
[30] Prov. 18:21 (KJV)

the gospel so that everything is about us and not about fulfilling the commands of the gospel.

Behind every great lie is a great truth. Interwoven with every great deception is a great principle. Behind every mystery is an answer. Baptists have great doctrine, strong faith, and biblical training, but some groups can take the cessationist theory too far and almost eliminate the Holy Spirit. On the other end of the spectrum, you have great groups that really focus on the Holy Spirit, but then can get sidetracked focusing on signs, wonders, and manifestations, some of which might not be of God. Likewise, the prosperity gospel has taken their truths, grasped their realities, and twisted them to their destruction.

> The greedy materialism of the prosperity gospel turns the biblical gospel on its head. The true gospel is an offer of salvation from sin and spiritual death. The prosperity gospel ignores those eternal realities and falsely promises deliverance from temporal problems like financial poverty and physical sickness. Jesus called his disciples to abandon all, take up their crosses, and follow him (Luke 9:23). By contrast, the prosperity gospel offers carnal comforts, earthly riches, and worldly success to millions of desperate people who literally buy into it. Whereas the true gospel centers on the Glory of God, the prosperity gospel puts man's wants and desires front and center.[31]

> I am talking about power, not to fall on the ground and shake like a worm, not power to claim a Mercedes Benz, not power to say you healed somebody when, in fact, he didn't get healed. I am talking about the power to live the Christian life, the power to walk in sacrificial love, the power to pray down strongholds, the power to preach the Gospel. That is what I am talking about. That is what we need.[32]

These are spots in your feasts of charity, when they feast with

---

[31] Macarthur, John F. *Strange Fire - The Danger of Offending the Holy Spirit with Counterfeit Wor*. Thomas Nelson, 2013, 52.
[32] Paul Washer, *Empowered by the Holy Spirit*, HeartCry Missionary, Aug 12, 2009.

you, feeding themselves without fear: clouds they are without water, carried about of winds; trees whose fruit withereth, without fruit, twice dead, plucked up by the roots; Raging waves of the sea, foaming out their own shame; wandering stars, to whom is reserved the blackness of darkness for ever.[33]

Albert Mohler stated: Prosperity theology is a false gospel. Its message is unbiblical and its promises fail. God never assures his people of material abundance or physical health. Instead, Christians are promised the riches of Christ, the gift of eternal life, and the assurance of glory in the eternal presence of the living God."[34]

A Pastor should be compelled by love, not treasure and glory. Twisting scriptures for self-enrichment is how these "pastors" finance their jets, mansions, boats, sports cars, and Armani suits. The first twist is subtle, and you don't even need to be a rich prosperity pastor to indulge in it. It is that if you give money to this preacher, God is going to give money to you. Kind of like an imaginary 401k or stock market dividend. They will find someone in the church that got a raise and prop them up on stage. If you give enough money, you can get a raise also. Desperate people believe this, then they give their money away, then they have less money, become more desperate, and the pastor tells them they didn't give enough or have enough faith when they gave, rendering the giving useless, and they need to regive even more money with better faith this time. When your prosperity pastor tells you that you need to give him a portion of your salary to upgrade his jet, something Kenneth Copeland and Jesse Duplantis really did, tell him: "A fool and his money are soon departed." Once the concept of giving money to greed so greed can replicate more greed is established, it is an open door to create more wealth and deceive.

---

[33] 1 Jude 12-13 (KJV)
[34] Hinn, Costi W. *God, Greed, and the (Prosperity) Gospel: How Truth Overwhelms a Life Built on Lies*. Grand Rapids, MI: Zondervan, 2019, **86**.

They then introduce the hundred fold concept, that if you give one dollar to them you will get one hundred back. If you give 10,000 you will get 1,000,000 back. Then if you reinvest that million, you get 100 million back. Just invest that 100 million in the imaginary Godmarket and you get 10 billion back. Invest that back and you get one trillion dollars. One last check to write to Kenneth Copeland and now you can pay off the U.S. national debt, buy a country or two, and have money left over for yourself. Neat idea, and this is surely ahead of throwing your money in the bank or stock market and collecting a little interest, and even better than buying Amazon stock back when it was a bookstore. The concept comes from when Isaac was told to go to the land that God told him and not go into Egypt. This might not have made sense at first, as all of the wealth is in Egypt, but Isaac listened as he was told: "Sojourn in this land, and I will be with thee, and will bless thee; for unto thee, and unto thy seed, I will give all these countries, and I will perform the oath which I sware unto Abraham thy father."[35] Isaac got a good start. "Because Abraham obeyed my voice, and kept my charge, my commandements, my statutes, and my laws."[36] Later in Genesis we find: "Then Isaac sowed in the land, and received in the same year an hundredfold: and the Lord blessed him."[37] A one hundred fold return on the land was a huge blessing of the day, even more so during famine time. Usual returns were generally not this high. According to John Gill's exposition of the Bible on this verse, there have been other instances of larger returns: "Herodotus speaks of a country, near to the place where the Euphrates runs into the Tigris, on which the city Ninus was, which nowhere failed of producing two hundred fold, and the better sort of it even three hundred."[38] Under prosperity theology thinking, if you send your money to Iraq you can get a 300% return on it.

---

[35] Gen. 26:3 (KJV)
[36] Gen. 26:5 (KJV)
[37] Gen. 26:12 (KJV)
[38] "Genesis 26:12 - Commentary & Verse Meaning - Bible." Bible Study Tools. Accessed March 9, 2020. https://www.biblestudytools.com/commentaries/gills-exposition-of-the-bible/genesis-26-12.html.

But notice how Isaac earned the hundred fold: he followed the voice of God, did what he was supposed to do, and went where he was supposed to go. He was also blessed through the righteousness of his father who followed God's commandments and laws. He did not offer up a bunch of grain and sheep at the local mega church.

The next thing the prosperity teachers will try to do is tie into the Abrhamic covenant. "I will make my covenant between Me and you, and will multiply you exceedingly. . . you shall be a father of many nations. . . I will make you exceedingly fruitful; and I will make nations of you, and kings shall come from you."[39] A few chapters earlier we have: "I will bless you And make your name great; And you shall be a blessing. I will bless those who bless you, And I will curse him who curses you; And in you all the families of the earth shall be blessed."[40] Prosperity teacher's tie into the Abrahamic covenant as a way to establish wealth for themselves. The issue with the Abrahamic covenant is not whether a covenant with Abraham is even applicable to us, that theological topic will be skipped. You can walk around your house speaking this declaration over yourself and legally change your name to Abraham and plan to pay child support for all your descendants. It is important to note that God made his covenant with Abraham for being a righteous man, a man that followed God's commandments so diligently that he was even willing to sacrifice his only son, a sacrifice that God himself eventually had to make. While Abraham made numerous sacrifices, including that of his livestock, he never offered grain to the local priests in return for more grain. He was blessed for his obedience and his righteousness.

The prosperity gospel uses various tricks and techniques to increase wealth for itself. The idea of giving to an organization to get health and wealth from God is paramount to its success. They will tie into the Abrahamic covenant or use other stories and examples tied in with

---

[39] Gen. 17:2-6 (NKJV)
[40] Gen. 12:2-3 (NKJV)

cherry picked verses. The idea that by giving to them you will get one hundred times as much back, is one key component. For many in the movement, that tie financial prosperity to spirituality, they go as far as saying wealthy people are blessed by God and the poor are cursed. Some will say giving to their particular ministry will result in a special anointing for you, and tell you to not give to the poor, as you will not receive as much harvest. This of course contradicts: "Blessed is he who considers the poor; The Lord will deliver him in time of trouble. The Lord will preserve him and keep him alive, And he will be blessed on the earth;"[41] Gimmicks such as special anointed prayer cloths or other items are oftentimes sold. Or people are told that giving on a certain day will increase the blessing. Some in the circles encourage members to give out of debt and God will provide supernatural debt cancellation. Concepts such as "naming your seed" and "double portions" are tossed around. Some go as far as to say Christ didn't die for your atonement, but for your financial gain. While these tricks and techniques may use parts of the gospel to hook its prey, it is important to note, they are not the gospel.

In her book *Blessed*, Kate Bowler makes a distinction between "hard" prosperity teachers such as EW Kenyon, Oral Roberts, Kennith Hagin, and Kenneth Copeland and those under soft prosperity such as Joel Osten and Joyce Meyers. Kate details how Faith teachers dubbed each prayer, tithe, word, emotion, or action a "seed" whose spiritual consequences have not come into season.[42] "Some churches kept detailed financial reports on their members, even asking them to submit tax records to verify that they paid their full tithes."[43] George Bloomer divided his Durham based Bethel Family Worship Center congregation into lines come tithing time, a $10 line, a $50 line, a $100 line, etc.[44] Joel Osteen has a

---

[41] Psalm 41:1-2A (NKJV)
[42] Bowler, Kate. *Blessed: a History of the American Prosperity Gospel*. New York: Oxford University Press, 2018, 67.
[43] Ibid., 98.
[44] Ibid., 132.

ministry mascot champ, with four arms, antennae sprouting from his head, and tennis shoes, emphasizing the church message", "Discover the Champion in You."[45] "Meyer's lasting appeal lay in her ability to balance the victory of the prosperity message with the reality of emotional hardships."[46] The tithe no longer becomes the gift of a cheerful giver, but an obligation expected for divine blessings.

Prosperity preachers tell their congregants that if they give them money, they will get money in return from God. And of course financial opportunities are there for the taking, for the heathen and the Christian, especially in America in the Land of Opportunity, in a rising economy. However, the congregants would be financially better if they kept their money and invested it in Real Estate, the stock market, a 401k, The Kingdom of God, the bank, or even buried in the ground. The idea of faith and prayer are also twisted around outside of their true intentions. Instead of praying for "Thy will be done" adherents, make declarations about their wealth and health to force God to comply with their demands. Faith is no longer about the promises of God and faith for God's will in our lives, but rather faith that you will be rich and can upgrade your Honda to a Bentley. Ironically, the only people driving Bentleys at the prosperity churches are the pastors; many of the congregants are left changing their own oil in their Toyotas to save a dollar.

Throughout history, there have been groups and divisions of people that have rid themselves of all material wealth and intentionally lived in extreme poverty as a way of drawing closer to God. Other groups have added in other physical torments such as flagellations, or sleep and food deprivation. But outside of fasting, which is Biblical, none of these items are Biblical mandates. If you are poor, it would make sense to make simple practical changes to no longer be poor. Giving your money away to people on TV is not going to help in this endeavor, as you will just have the same

---

[45] Ibid., 191.
[46] Ibid., 195.

amount of money that you had before, minus the amount that you just gave. The rich have to contend with: It is "Easier for a camel to go through a needle's eye, than for a rich man to enter into the kingdom of God,"[47] Fortunately it later says: "The things which are impossible with men are possible with God."[48] Someone in America who lives in a two-bedroom, one-bath, one-car garage house in a non-affluent area and is struggling to make ends meet might be considered poor by a wealthy man in the city over by American standards, but this same poor person could be considered rich by global standards, as many across the world do not have food and a roof over their head, let alone a roof over their car. Agur from Proverbs said: "Remove far from me vanity and lies: give me neither poverty nor riches; feed me with food convenient for me: Lest I be full, and deny thee, and say, Who is the Lord? or lest I be poor, and steal, and take the name of my God in vain."[49] Money itself seems to be amoral, but the love of money which can sometimes impact the poor as much as the rich, is the root of all evil. Millions have died under empires that have jostled for economic power and ruthless businesses have taken advantage of the poor countless times for more money. It is the love and the constant chasing of money, putting earthly treasures in front of heavenly treasures that is the problem as "No one can serve two masters, for either he will hate the one and love the other, or he will be devoted to the one and despise the other. You cannot serve God and money."[50] Any person can take an inventory of their life and see if it is invested in houses, cars, and toys or in Heavenly treasure. Oftentimes we fall short and need to repent and make changes, that is a part of life. The Bible shows us that something must be first.

Many things are good in moderation but can be ruined by taking them to extremes. BBQ, ice cream, and thick steaks taste great and should

---

[47] Luke 18:25 (KJV)
[48] Luke 18:27 (KJV)
[49] Prov. 30:8-9 (KJV)
[50] Matt. 6:24 (ESV)

be enjoyed, but if you spend all year feasting on these items, you will be obese and it will lead to gluttony. Vacations, breaks, and pleasure are nice and can provide recuperation, but if you spend your entire life just chasing pleasure and vacation, you have missed the point. Prayer is great, but if you spend your whole life praying and never take the action that God has for you, you will not break into the kingdom work that God has for your life. Likewise, financial advice and promises are littered throughout the Bible, God can deliver you from financial bondage such as debt. Making money can be used for good, But making money and producing income are not the point of life or the point of the Bible. Everything in the Bible points to the Cross, either in the Old Testament that points to his coming or the New Testament that shares the results. And 2,000 years of Christian history may have been littered with various theological views, but traditional Christian theology has been consistent that Christ died on the Cross as a blood atonement for your sins, not for financial gain. In many cases it might not be wrong to enjoy some of the many pleasures that we have in America, what is wrong is to manipulate the gospel to support those pleasures. In these types of churches, The church has abandoned the Almighty, and bowed their knee to the almighty dollar.

Healing is the second aspect the prosperity preachers drive home. Isiaiah says: "But he was wounded for our transgressions, he was bruised for our iniquities: the chastisement of our peace was upon him; and with his stripes we are healed."[51] John Scofield notes in his study Bible that: "The Lord took away the diseases of men by healing them. He died for our sins, not for our diseases. For physical disease in itself is not sin; it is merely one of the results of sin."[52] This section from Matthew does seem to imply physical healing was included in the atonement when he quotes

---

[51] Isa. 53:5 (KJV)
[52] Hassan, Riaz. *Scofield Study Bible: King James Version, Black Bonded Leather*. Place of publication not identified: Oxford University Press, 2003, **944**.

Isaiah: "That it might be fulfilled which was spoken by Esaias the prophet, saying, Himself took our infirmities, and bare our sicknesses."[53] Peter brings it back to the thrust of the cross by saying: "Who his own self bare our sins in his own body on the tree, that we, being dead to sins, should live unto righteousness: by whose stripes ye were healed."[54] Prosperity faith healers use these verses to guarantee health on this earth. Dr. J Vernon Mcgee states that: "To contend that healing is in the Atonement is beside the point. So is a glorified body in the Atonement, but I don't have mine yet. Do you? . . . Why did Paul urge Timothy to take a little wine for his stomach? Why didn't he urge him to get his healing in the Atonement?"[55] John MacArthur stated: "Those who claim that Christians should never be sick because there is healing in the atonement should also claim that Christians should never die, because Jesus also conquered death in the atonement. The central message of the gospel is deliverance from sin. It is the good news about forgiveness, not health. Christ has made sin, not disease, and He died on the cross for our sin, not our sickness."[56]

Regardless of your theological view on what happened on the cross, the central intent of the cross was the atonement of our sins. Jesus Christ physically healed people in the Bible and Jesus Christ physically heals people today. But nowhere in scripture did people have to pay for their physical healing. If you want to tie physical healing to the atonement, then why would you then pay someone else for that healing, the work was already done. Giving money to a prosperity pastor is not going to help your physical health, it will only hurt your bank account. To the desperate widow dying of cancer that is thinking of giving her life savings to the

---

[53] Matt. 8:17 (KJV)
[54] 1 Pet. 2:24 (KJV)
[55] McGee, J. Vernon. *Thru the Bible with J. Vernon McGee (Vol. 4, Matthew - Romans)*. Nashville: T. Nelson, 1981, 49.
[56] By. "Are We Physically Healed by Jesus' Stripes?" Grace to You, August 5, 2019. https://www.gty.org/library/blog/B160817.

prosperity preacher to heal her of this pain, now you will be broke on top of dying of cancer. Christ can heal and he does heal, but the people on TV, cannot. One might think, "But I am giving it to the Lord." You are not giving it to the Lord. You are giving to fund mansions, yachts, institutions, and egos. A wiser, more Godly use of the money would be to just write a check to Jeff Bezos so he can improve the efficiency of getting packages to your door or something, not fund false doctrine AntiChrist to God's doctrine. Facing a terminal illness can make people desperate, it is the main source of cash that feeds the prosperity preachers. Sending money to the guy on TV is not going to help, but actually turning to the heart of God through faith and prayer could, or at the very least learn to walk hand in hand with the Father who will walk along with you through the process. Turning to God should not be done to gain wealth or solve all of your problems, though turning to God and prayer may very well cure your illness, provide financial miracles, and see deliverance. But what will happen when you run into the sickness, when you run into financial problems, when your child becomes sick, is that now you are not alone, you will have someone that is walking with you, encouraging you, and sometimes carrying you along.

> Beware of false prophets, which come to you in sheep's clothing, but inwardly they are ravening wolves. Ye shall know them by their fruits. Do men gather grapes of thorns, or figs of thistles? Even so every good tree bringeth forth good fruit; but a corrupt tree bringeth forth evil fruit. A good tree cannot bring forth evil fruit, neither can a corrupt tree bringeth forth good fruit. Every tree that bringeth not forth good fruit is hewn down, and cast into the fire. Wherefore by their fruits ye shall know them. Not every one that saith unto me, Lord, Lord, shall enter into the kingdom of heaven; but he that doeth the will of my Father which is in heaven. Many will say to me in that day, Lord, Lord, have we not prophesied in thy name? and in thy name have cast out devils? and in thy name done many

wonderful works? And then will I profess unto them, I never knew you: depart from me, ye that work iniquity.[57]

Of course, false prophets don't advertise themselves as hypocritical heretics. They come in sheep's clothing, masquerade as angels of light, and promise liberty to others while they themselves are enslaved to sinful lusts . . . Given enough time, false prophets will inevitably evidence their true nature in how they live.[58]

When we get the sovereignty of God wrong, we get God wrong. When we get the abundant life wrong, we get Jesus wrong. When we get faith and confession wrong, we get salvation wrong. Why is that a huge deal? Because all roads that the prosperity gospel paves lead to hell."[59]

One of the cruelest lies of contemporary 'faith healers' is that the people they fail to heal are guilty of sinful unbelief, a lack of faith, or 'negative confession.'[60]

Viewed their relationship to God as a give-and-get transaction. They saw God as a kind of sugar daddy who existed to make them healthy, wealthy, and happy on account of service rendered. While God certainly does provide and care for His followers, the Prosperity Gospel is a corruption of His self-revelation and a distortion of His plan of redemption . . . [61] Instead of promising Christ, this gospel promises health and wealth . . . [62] The prosperity message can be and often is preached without Jesus."[63]

Costi Hinn wrote two books detailing the deception he found in the church in the prosperity community when he worked directly for his

---

[57] Matt. 7:15-23, (KJV)
[58] Macarthur, John F. *Strange Fire - The Danger of Offending the Holy Spirit with Counterfeit Wor*. Thomas Nelson, 2013, **106-107**.
[59] Hinn, Costi W. *God, Greed, and the (Prosperity) Gospel: How Truth Overwhelms a Life Built on Lies*. Grand Rapids, MI: Zondervan, 2019, **100**.
[60] **Quote is from John Macarthur taken from:** Hinn, Costi W. *God, Greed, and the (Prosperity) Gospel: How Truth Overwhelms a Life Built on Lies*. Grand Rapids, MI: Zondervan, 2019, **131**.
[61] Jones, David W., and Russell S. Woodbridge. *Health, Wealth, and Happiness: How the Prosperity Gospel Overshadows the Gospel of Christ*. Grand Rapids, MI: Kregel Publications, 2017, **8**.
[62] Ibid., 17.
[63] Ibid., 44.

uncle Benny Hinn and saw the corruption of the prosperity movement first hand. Costi gives us first hand accounts of how vast volumes of the poor in India would give what little that they had under the guise of healing so their uncle could spend the night in gold-plated hotels. He concluded that: "I wanted to be a real pastor, shepherding the flock in faithfulness and not for selfish gain."[64] Since publishing his first book he has "received emails, tweets, and Facebook messages from people all over the world. These people explained how their lives had been devastated as a result of my uncle's life and ministry."[65]

While most churches will not go as far to say that Jesus died on the cross for your financial gain or that Jesus was some type of billionaire businessman, many do subtly twist the idea that if you give them a few more dollars, God is going to bless you a few more times. The idea that you can earn your way into God's favor is permeating Christianity. Previously, we had indulgences, the catholic empire, and the idea of spending money to earn your eternal salvation. Today we have tithes, the prosperity empire, and the idea of spending money to earn favor with God. The concept that you can buy your way into financial favor with God or receive curses due to your lack thereof, is the same works-based system that Luther fought and risked his life against. They both are antichrist to God's system which is "For God so loved the world, that he gave his only begotten Son, that whosoever believeth in him should not perish, but have everlasting life."[66] This system leads to salvation, freedom, love, and truth.

---

[64] Hinn, Costi W. *God, Greed, and the (Prosperity) Gospel: How Truth Overwhelms a Life Built on Lies.* Grand Rapids, MI: Zondervan, 2019, **148.**
[65] Ibid., 149.
[66] John 3:16 (KJV)

III. The Compromised Church

Prophetical events have taken place that may put us in or near the end times. Many are looking for the Antichrist, but not the falling away that precedes it. Paul, during his address to the church of Thessalonica, made it clear that before the man of sin shows up, there is going to be a great falling away: "Let no man deceive you by any means: for that day shall not come, except there come a falling away first, and that man of sin be revealed, the son of perdition."[67] You have to be careful of pinning down Eschatological events, as it will happen as "A thief in the night."[68] There is a good chance that we might be living in the age of the great falling away, if we continue in this direction.

False teaching, deception, and apostasy are mentioned in every New Testament book outside of Philemon. It is one of the main battles that the Apostle Paul and Jesus Christ deal with. "And Jesus answered and said unto them, Take heed that no man deceive you. For many shall come in my name, saying, I am Christ; and shall deceive many." [69] Paul warns Timothy: "Now the Spirit speaketh expressly, that in the latter times some shall depart from the faith, giving heed to seducing spirits, and doctrines

---

[67] 2 Thess. 2:3, (KJV)
[68] 1 Thess. 5:2b, (YLT)
[69] Matt. 24: 4-5., (KJV)

of devils."[70] Also: "But there were false prophets also among the people, even as there shall be false teachers among you, who privily shall bring in damnable heresies, even denying the Lord that bought them, and bring upon themselves swift destruction."[71] Finally: "For there shall arise false Christs, and false prophets, and shall shew great signs and wonders; insomuch that, if it were possible, they shall deceive the very elect."[72]

The church and Christian faith need to be built upon sound and unchanging doctrinal pillars. "Whosoever transgresseth, and abideth not in the doctrine of Christ, hath not God. He that abideth in the doctrine of Christ, he hath both the Father and the Son. If there come any unto you and bring not this doctrine, receive him not into your house, neither bid him God speed."[73] And: "That we may be no longer children, tossed to and fro and carried about with every wind of doctrine, by the sleight of men, in craftiness, after the wiles of error"[74] In the Compromised Churches of today, there is a move to remove denominational titles, doctrines, and even the name "church." Doctrinal substance appears less and less in children's programs or presented from the pulpit. Many churches now frown upon anything that is fundamental doctrinally. If the word "Doctrine is taken from the Bible, then the doctrines of God can be completely eliminated."[75]

We do not have to guess at how God would run a church because he has already shown us in the Bible. The New Testament church format and formula for growth is clearly outlined through the New Testament. Acts and other books detail the rampant growth of the church amidst heavy persecution. It would seem as if the early church was destined to fail, when all of the major participants of the movement were beaten,

---

[70] 1 Tim. 4:1., (KJV)
[71] 2 Pet. 2:1-3., (KJV)
[72] Matt. 24:24., (KJV)
[73] 2 John 1:9-10 (KJV)
[74] Eph. 4:14 (ASV)
[75] Hutchings, N. W. *The Dark Side of the Purpose Driven Church*. Crane, MO: Defender Pub., 2011., p. 72.

killed, or exiled. Interestingly enough, that did not happen and the church experienced its most powerful growth during this time period. Other periods of revival in church history were in 1517 when Martin Luther attacked the corrupt Catholic Church who also prevented their people from accessing the Bible. Martin Luther's Reformation was based on "Solo Scriptures" Scripture Only, and started by him posting his 95 Theses on the Wittenberg chapel. The Americas saw powerful revivals in the 20th century led by Jonathan Edwards and George Whitefield. These revivals changed the landscape of America so drastically that they are even noted by many secular historians.

These movements that led to thousands of lives being transformed and corrected the direction of the church all had something in common, and that is that they had as their foundation the Word of God or the teachings of Christ. The church needs to return to the word of God, prayer, and the fear of God, which is an acknowledgement that there is sin and man needs to repent, which is the foundation of the gospel. The new church formed after the death of Christ did not even invite seekers to the services, let alone structure the services for them, as they were meant for the believers. They strengthened the lives of the members so they could transform lives.

Deception is the fuel that feeds the fire of the Compromised Church. Today in Compromised Churches across America, pastors get up in the pulpit, craft a generic self-improvement message about being a good person, and sprinkle in a half-dozen Bible verses from a half-dozen Bible versions. Many used paraphrased versions of the Bible which actively waters down the source of truth. The prince of preachers, Charles Spurgeon, stated:

> The idea of a progressive gospel seems to have fascinated many. To us that notion is sort of cross-breed between nonsense and blasphemy. After the gospel has been found effectual in the eternal salvation of untold multitudes, it

seems rather late in the day to alter it; and, since it is the revelation of the all-wise and unchanging God, it appears somewhat audacious to attempt its improvement."[76]

The book of Hosea tells us that: "My people are destroyed for lack of knowledge: because thou hast rejected knowledge, I will also reject thee, that thou shalt be no priest to me: seeing thou hast forgotten the law of thy God, I will also forget thy children."[77] When the world is mixed in with the church, it results in weak or little to no faith in Jesus Christ. The new powerless gospel talks about God's love and his plan for your life but says nothing about repentance, recognition of guilt and the penalty of death for sins, or the sacrifice of Christ on the cross. "The gospel is the death, burial, and resurrection of Jesus for our sins. It is not a message of convenience or embarrassment ... We are not saying that you must preach fire and brimstone all the time. But the fact is the gospel that offends no one is not the gospel of the Bible."[78] The book of Jude warns us: "For there are certain men crept in unawares, who were before of old ordained to this condemnation, ungodly men, turning the grace of our God into lasciviousness, and denying the only Lord God, and our Lord Jesus Christ. [79] Paul warns us: "But though we, or an angel from heaven, preach any other gospel unto you than that which we have preached unto you, let him be accursed. As we said before, so say I now again, If any man preach any other gospel unto you than that ye have received, let him be accursed."[80]

Some churches believe that they provide substance because they provide free coffee and doughnuts. But this is not the substance people need. "Simple obedience to the Word of God is being ignored, as the church has become more a place of human interest rather than the place

---

[76] Ibid., 31.
[77] Hosea 4:6, KJV
[78] Billy Lauderdale, *An Apostate Church.* Lexington, KY: 2016., p. 50-51.
[79] Jude 1:4 (KJV)
[80] Gal. 1:8-9 (KJV)

to pursue the Kingdom of God."[81] When the church is more concerned about competing with Hollywood, rather than focusing on the Word of God, you are going to have a problem. When the church is more concerned about creating members rather than disciples, you are going to have a problem. When the church is more concerned about the growth of the church, rather than the growth of its sheep, you are going to have a problem. "It is a solemn thing, and no small scandal in the kingdom, to see God's children starving while actually seated at the Father's table."[82]

I have had the opportunity to spend years of my life traveling. I have been to churches in Fairbanks down to Florida. From Maine to Hawaii. I have been to a Morman church in Utah, A Catholic Church in Canada, and with Jehovah's Witnesses in Hawaii. I have been to small churches and large churches, wealthy churches and struggling churches. Spanish-speaking churches and English-speaking churches. Black Pentecostal churches with upbeat rhythm and dancing and white Baptist churches that calmly sung hymns. Churches that delivered a message without emotion, and churches that carried so much emotion people were bouncing around. Minor doctrinal differences, beliefs, cultures, sizes, and styles of worship would be present at all the churches.

But a pattern quickly developed. There were those churches that adhered to the Word of God and based the church policies, ideas, and preaching from the Bible, the teachings of Christ, and traditional Biblical doctrine, and then there were those that would not. Opinions and methodologies would differ between the churches, but they were united under this front. Most of the people in the Bible-based churches were generally active in the community, brought more people into the fellowship, evangelized to other people, personally read the Bible at home, and generally had healthier families and spiritual lives. The other groups

---

[81] Covarrubias, Loren. *Why is the Devil in My Garden?* Waterford, MI: Call from the Mountain Media, 2011. p.122
[82] Tozer, A.W. *The Pursuit of God*. Abbotsford, WI: Aneko Press, 2015. p.x.

would occasionally do a few of these things, but most of the time was spent on activities that would glorify the institution. The people were generally not active in the community and, in many unfortunate cases, the home life was falling apart, the Bible did not have a prominent place, and you rarely saw genuinely changed lives. Most attended sporadically, and the regular church attenders were locked in through a church job or volunteer activity. These churches would rely on marketing to draw people in and generally kept them there through busy work volunteer-type activities, control, or let them build their own religious legacy through the institution. "They minister constantly to believers who feel within their breasts a longing which their teaching simply does not satisfy."[83]

Hollywood, or the film industry, does about 43 billion dollars in business per year.[84] Most homes have a TV, many have multiple TV's, and some reports say some Americans watch as much as 40 hours of television per week.[85] Watching TV is a regular full time job for some. Devices entertain, amuse, and indoctrinate. Americans are getting hooked on entertainment, and it is a part of the culture. The church has seen this, and some churches are trying to compete with Hollywood. Using entertainment to educate in the church is not the problem. The problem is when the church sees its primary purpose to entertain. And when it does, it will find that it will fall short of Hollywood, but more importantly, it will fall short of its true purpose.

One issue that quickly became problematic in many Compromised Churches was the idea of evangelization. It seemed as if once the gospel started getting hidden in the Sunday morning churches, the people also

---

[83] Ibid., x.
[84] Robb, David. "U.S. Film Industry Topped $43 Billion In Revenue Last Year, Study Finds, But It's Not All Good News." Deadline. https://deadline.com/2018/07/film-industry-revenue-2017-ibisworld-report-gloomy-box-office-1202425692/ (accessed Feb. 6, 2020)
[85] Madrigal, Alexa. "When Did T.V. Watching Peak." The Atlantic. https://www.theatlantic.com/technology/archive/2018/05/when-did-tv-watching-peak/561464/ (accessed Feb. 6, 2020).

hid it from the community. The book of Matthew concludes with this command, commonly known as the great commission: "Go therefore and make disciples of all the nations, baptizing them in the name of the Father and of the Son and of the Holy Spirit, teaching them to observe all things that I have commanded you; and lo, I am with you always, even to the end of the age. Amen."[86] While all of the gospels retell the same story from each of their own first-hand accounts and perspectives, they all include the great commission. Mark tells it like this at the end of his account: "Go ye into all the world, and preach the gospel to every creature. He that believeth and is baptized shall be saved; but he that believeth not shall be damned."[87] The Acts of the Apostles starts with: "But you shall receive power, after that the Holy Ghost is come upon you: and ye shall be witnesses unto me both in Jerusalem, and in all Judaea, and in Samaria, and unto the uttermost part of the earth."[88] And also details what they did: "And daily in the temple, and in every house, they ceased not to teach and preach Jesus Christ."[89] "When Silas and Timothy arrived from Macedonia, Paul was occupied with the word, testifying to the Jews that the Christ was Jesus."[90] Then later in the book: "For he powerfully refuted the Jews in public, demonstrating by the Scriptures that Jesus was the Christ."[91] And the Acts of the Apostles concludes with: "And Paul dwelt two whole years in his own hired house, and received all that came in unto him, Preaching the kingdom of God, and teaching those things which concern the Lord Jesus Christ, with all confidence, no man forbidding him."[92] Paul's prison epistle to the Philippians talks about some people preaching Christ out of envy and strife, others out of love and good will: "Knowing that I am set for the defence of the gospel. What then? Notwithstanding, every way,

---

[86] Matt. 28:19-20 (NKJV)
[87] Mark 16:15-16 (KJV)
[88] Acts 1:8 (KJV)
[89] Acts 5:42 (KJV)
[90] Acts 18:5 (ESV)
[91] Acts 18:28 (KJV)
[92] Acts 28: 30-31 (KJV)

whether in pretence, or in truth, Christ is preached; and I therein do rejoice, yea, and will rejoice."[93] And Corinthians tells us: "For what we proclaim is not ourselves, but Jesus Christ as Lord, with ourselves as your servants for Jesus' sake.[94]

Based on these verses and others, It would seem as if spreading the gospel was an important concept to Jesus and his disciples. After all, even though these people came from all different walks of life, fishermen, a carpenter, and a tax collector, they were all unified in dedicating, risking, and ultimately sacrificing their time and lives for the gospel. Paul went to great lengths to spread this message, stating: "From the Jews five times I received forty stripes minus one. Three times I was beaten with rods; once I was stoned; three times I was shipwrecked; a night and a day I have been in the deep; in journeys often, in perils of waters, in perils of robbers, in perils of my own countrymen, in perils of the Gentiles, in perils in the city, in perils in the wilderness, in perils in the sea, in perils among false brethren; in weariness and toil, in sleeplessness often, in hunger and thirst, in fastings often, in cold and nakedness."[95] But according to a 2018 Barna poll, almost half of practicing Christian Millenials say evangelism is wrong.

According to another Gallop poll conducted Dec. 11-14, 2004, Americans have nine "close friends," not including their relatives. This includes 45% of Americans who say they have six or more close friends, 39% who have between three and five close friends, and 14% who have one or two close friends. Only 2% of Americans say they have no close friends. "Seventy-three percent of Americans are satisfied with the number of friends they have, and only 27% would like to have more friends."

---

[93] Phil. 1:17b-18 (KJV)
[94] 2 Cor. 4:5 (NKJV)
[95] 2 Cor. 11:24-27(NKJV)

In the hustle and bustle of today's Americanized society, the 27% that say they would like to have more friends probably don't have the time to sustain and nurture more close friendships. Many families have two full-time working parents, and free time is spent racing kids from one sporting, school, or social activity to the next. Single-parent families are the new normal, and all the responsibilities that were traditionally split between two parents are now heaped onto one parent. Cell phones and the digital age could have been used to create more free time, but instead they allow the businessperson to accomplish more work and take on more responsibilities. It is rare today to find someone that has enough money, but it is even rarer to find someone that has enough time. Upon reaching adulthood, most people already have a group of friends that they have nurtured based on various social interests, athletics, or schooling.

Out of this society birthed a new idea called friendship evangelism. There seems to be two arms with the movement. One technique revolves around living a life so amazing that people see how great you are, and are converted, without the need to even share the gospel. The other arm of the movement focuses on befriending people prior to sharing the truth. And there is truth to this; communicating properly and being friendly with people is certainly more effective than angrily yelling at them. But there are problems with this. When seeker churches wait until Wednesday night to present the Gospel message so they do not offend believers on Sundays, many times the message gets left behind. And when churches encourage people to wait for the right and perfect time to spread the gospel, oftentimes the message gets left behind.

Jesus sent clear instructions on how to evangelize to people with a simple message: "Repent: for the kingdom of heaven is at hand."[96] We are told that we should be prepared to witness for the faith: "But sanctify the Lord God in your hearts: and be ready always to give an answer to every

---

[96] Matt. 4:17 (KJV)

man that asketh you a reason of the hope that is in you with meekness and fear."[97] The target audience is here: "Go therefore, and teach all nations, baptizing them in the name of the Father, and of the Son, and of the Holy Ghost."[98] The message might not seem to be needed to those who do not have it, as someone with undiagnosed cancer may not know yet that he needs to get rid of the cancer. "For the preaching of the cross is to them that perish foolishness; but unto us which are saved it is the power of God."[99] "But we preach Christ crucified, unto the Jews a stumbling block, and unto the Greeeks foolishness."[100] The main problem with churches relying on marketing to recruit, rather than having members evangelize are the results. People will be drawn to institutions and recruited as if it were a political party, but people will not be recruited to the Kingdom of Christ.

Intentional evangelization has been used before. Jesus and a relatively small band stood in stark contrast to the power of the Roman Empire and changed the known world at the time. The Great Awakenings shook and recreated the fabric and culture of America. Countless missionaries pierced tribes and groups across the World. Livingstone, Graham, Spurgeon, Edwards, Finney, Elliot, Whitefield, Sunday, and others used the simple gospel message to change souls, families, and countries. And maybe these people would have led a few people to Christ using friendship evangelism if they had time, but they were too busy leading thousands and tens of thousands to Christ. I am not aware of a great evangelist, person, or church that has successfully used this technique for the multitudes. For every recruit that is pulled in front of the church as a trophy to the technique, scores of souls are missed. "Clearly, the biblical method of evangelism is the faithful proclamation of the truth of Scripture in conjunction with the living testimony of those

---

[97] 1 Pet. 3:15 (KJV)
[98] Matt. 28:19 (KJV)
[99] 1 Cor. 1:17-28 (KJV)
[100] I Cor. 1:23 (KJV)

who have been changed by that truth. When Jesus went about teaching the gospel message of salvation, He taught love and forgiveness, being kind and compassionate. But he went to sinners in order to convict them of their sins . . . We are commissioned to bring the same message to the world, speaking the truth in love from a heart changed by the Savior"[101]

As Christianity was fueled by the gospel, Control is what fuels many Compromised Churches. Many pastors have set themselves up to be above the people, not of the people. Most pastors choose the profession to help people, but then find the power intoxicating and addicting. Absolute power corrupts absolutely. The main confusion comes in that they think that they are in control of the church; however, "Christ is the head of the church: and he is the saviour of the body."[102] These pastors most often start off with great intentions and an accountability system. Over time they are abandoned. Control, fear, and manipulation are oftentimes used to gain and maintain control over their empires. Self-picked elder boards and token individuals are used and dragged in front of the church to provide substance and support for the movement. Questioning the motives of the pastor will lead to ostracization, but unquestionable faith will earn that conditional love, and the opportunity to be used as a prop on the stage in the future.

The flag for control waves so large that it blocks out the light from above. You must resist the urge to relent to these pastors' unrelenting demand for loyalty and control. Do not bow your knee to them, do not allow them to take away your sins or provide your atonement; reserve that for the true King of Kings. Because for some, the ultimate goal, the reason for control, the reason they thirst for praise, is they are positioning themselves and angling themselves in front of God's position. They are

---

[101] "What is Friendship Evangelism?" Got Questions. www.gotquestions.org/friendship-evangelism.html (Accessed February 10, 2020).
[102] Ephesians 5:23 (KJV)

stealing his praise, his control, and his worship. This is not something new, Ezekial stated:

> The word of the LORD came to me: "Son of man, prophesy against the shepherds of Israel; prophesy and say to them: 'This is what the Sovereign LORD says: Woe to you shepherds of Israel who only take care of yourselves! Should not shepherds take care of the flock? You eat the curds, clothe yourselves with the wool and slaughter the choice animals, but you do not take care of the flock. You have not strengthened the weak or healed the sick or bound up the injured. You have not brought back the strays or searched for the lost. You have ruled them harshly and brutally. So they were scattered because there was no shepherd, and when they were scattered they became food for all the wild animals. My sheep wandered over all the mountains and on every high hill. They were scattered over the whole earth, and no one searched or looked for them. Therefore, you shepherds, hear the word of the LORD: As surely as I live, declares the Sovereign LORD, because my flock lacks a shepherd and so has been plundered and has become food for all the wild animals, and because my shepherds did not search for my flock but cared for themselves rather than for my flock, therefore, you shepherds, hear the word of the LORD: This is what the Sovereign LORD says: I am against the shepherds and will hold them accountable for my flock. I will remove them from tending the flock so that the shepherds can no longer feed themselves. I will rescue my flock from their mouths, and it will no longer be food for them."[103]

Love is important. It is an essential or the essential purpose of the faith. We have the Ten Commandments and others, then when Jesus was asked which of the commandments of the law was the greatest, he responded with: "Thou shalt love the Lord thy God with all thy heart, and with all thy soul, and with all thy mind. This is the first and greatest commandment. And the second is like unto it, Thou shalt love thy

---

[103] Ezekial 34: 1-10 (NIV)

neighbour as thyself. Of these two commandments hang all the law and the prophets."[104] Love is the primary thrust of the Christian faith, love God, love people. "If I give all I possess to the poor and give over my body to hardship that I may boast, but do not have love, I gain nothing."[105]

But even something as beautiful as Love can be twisted around by Compromised Churches, and conditional love can be confused with real love. Love can also be used to twist the truth.

> Nowhere in the scriptures does it say to abandon truth in order to love, But rather we are to speak the truth in love. It is truth that will set the lost free. To shy away from the truth because it brings scorn is to shine away from Jesus Christ himself as he is the truth... The reality is that you love yourself more than you love other people, which is why you don't care enough about them to share God's love. The cross takes the fire of God's judgment. God's wrath burned on him so we will be saved. Everyone will face judgment. The christian is supposed to be set apart... If you are not persecuted or hated, you are not preaching the truth, might be preaching water down stories, not the truth.[106]

However if you boil down the gospel message, you will find that there is more to it than just love. When discussing the Hawaiin culture he lives in, Pastor Matt Purvis stated:

> There are a lot of bad ideas of what Christ accomplished at the cross and his life, theories of the atonement or really bad ideas. There is the mystical idea of the atonement of Christ consciousness, that he can be found in the trees and the seas, prevalent in Hawaii. The concept that Christ's life, death, and resurrection is an example, an example to be a morally good person and we should follow that example. And then the Jesus died on the cross just to show you how much God loves you,

---

[104] Matthew 22:37-40 (KJV)
[105] I Corinthians 13:3 (NIV)
[106] Johnson, David. "The Law of the Lord is perfect." Sermon, Ocean View Evangelical Community Church, Ocean View Hawaii, February 17, 2019.

God loves you so much that there is no price he wouldn't pay to have you back, he was willing to give everything for us and in so by giving his son we will soften our hearts and bend our knees and say God I didn't know you loved me so much, I'm going to come to you now. There is some truth to it, but it still falls short of what Christ accomplished, in him we have redemption through his blood—the forgiveness of our trespasses according to the riches of his Grace . . . It goes far beyond showing us God's love, which is true . . . These other ideas are popular because they skip over our true condition . . . The good news is in Christ alone in him, not the idea of him.[107]

When churches start waving the flag for love, don't be foolishly mistaken and think you are going to start loving your neighbor as yourself or something, it is oftentimes a flag for conditional love, and there will be a price to pay.

Small groups can be used to strengthen the faith and provide fellowship. A good small group can be instrumental in changing lives and strengthening faith. But in many Compromised Churches, small groups are used not to solve any problems, but tie people closer to the problem. "Jesus was in a small group" is a catchy phrase. But Jesus didn't join a small group to play cards, small talk, and gossip about other church members. For some, small groups give the main church the ability to lock people into the system without having to personally shepherd the souls. In some cases the people sacrifice their family time, Bible Study time, careers, and free time, to read books on How to Make Friends and Influence People, instead of learning about Biblical commands. Make no mistake, when some churches start waving the flag for small groups, it is done to gain control and ensure income, not as a spiritual benefit to the members.

While there is always a balance to everything, and the constant beratement of people that they are sinners has been used in cases in the

---

[107] Purvis, Matt. "Ephesians - Aliens Welcome." Sermon, Grassroots Church, Pahoa, Hi, January 06, 2019.

past in an unacceptable way to judge and condemn, and an "anything goes" wild west approach to morality does not work either. The social acceptance of sin is taken to a new level in most if not all of the Compromised Churches. It is almost as if some think you get an extra prize for it. The "Do not judge lest you be judged" is used as a blanket endorsement for everything. You now have the benefit to fully indulge in whatever the sin of your fancy is. Or pick up some new ones while you are at it to better fit in with the culture of the church. Jokes are made about personal struggles that they are actually not really making any effort to quit. Sin that is allowed to grow and fester in your life or from past generations turns into bondage. Bondage wraps its tentacles around the believer's life and mind, and leads to a spiritual and sometimes physical death. Sin and bondages are now reclassified as medical conditions. Instead of repenting, prayer, fasting and turning to our Father in heaven to cleanse sin and bondages out of our lives and come out new, 12-step recovery programs are used or people are sent to the psychologists. The flag for sin will continuously wave in the background, as its removal threatens the religious environment, and makes people have to examine themselves.

Churches in the past have split over minor doctrinal differences or issues over petty arguments and power positions. This is wrong. In most cities, unifying a few churches would be beneficial, sharing the resources and being more effective and efficient. It is sad when churches split or argue about non-essential doctrinal differences. Now of course eliminating or radically changing the basic gospel message that has been in place for 2000 years is not a minor doctrinal difference. So when people start asking questions, the trumpet for unity will start to blare loudly, as the institution relies more on blind obedience rather than critical thinking. All of the versions of the Bible will be scoured, sermons will be crafted, the Pharisees and Sadducees will take arms, to fight the opposition. The flag for unity and conformity will be large and wide; they will passionately wave it and declare it before the institution, they will use it to rile support and stifle the opposition, they will be fighting for what they see as purpose, and in many cases it will trump the small flag for truth and the Cross of Christ.

The objective of this movement, like other cults and false religions, is to masquerade the message of the cross, to move its focus. America is running from the Christian principles it was once founded upon. Many of the churches across America have abandoned doctrine and embraced deception. Some say the greatest trick the devil ever pulled was convincing the world that he didn't exist. I think the greatest trick that he ever pulled was not getting God and the Bible out of society, but getting God and the Bible out of the Church.

The gospel message that Roman soldiers could not stop with their swords and spears was now voluntarily silenced across the American churches. Families, marriages, and teens were now getting destroyed and falling apart at a faster rate. Since the churches were no longer offering actual substance, they became institutions of self-help and support. The family flag was waved, saying everyone that conformed was part of the family. The love banner was waved, offering conditional love to those who would conform and align with the pattern. The Unity banner was waved, calling out to compromise and conform. Friendships were formed, patterns were developed, and people were brought together. Not to change lives, empower believers, or to stand strong against the world, but as a social network, a rotary club or a big boy scout group. Pastors that would not conform were ostracised from many churches, kicked out or gently removed to be less effective in smaller places. True believers were herded out and sent to wander and get wounded in different locations. Pastors seized greater power and put themselves in absolute god-like control to build empires unto themselves, at the expense of the sheep.

2,000 years ago, the religious people of the day took Jesus and had him hung on a tree. Jesus loved making fun of the religious people of the day, referring to them as a "Brood of vipers" and whitewashed tombs; he called them Pharisees and Saducess. When Jesus went to church, he caused trouble. One time, when he saw people selling items in God's church, he started flipping tables over. Today, selling trinkets and church swag in church is common. Today, if Jesus showed up in some of our Compromised Churches, he would be arrested, cast out, and probably assaulted. He just wouldn't quite conform or fit in with church culture. Later people that followed Jesus also found that they couldn't quite fit in with some churches. Martin Luther was thrown out by the Catholic Church. Johnathan Edwards, who helped lead the largest American Revival in History, was voted out of his church. George Whitefield often could not find churches willing to host him, so he would preach in fields, leading to the Great Awakening. The great reformer Jan Hus was burned at the stake by the church, and William Tyndale, the father of the English Bible, was both burned and strangled. While many churches have done and continue to do powerful works for the glory of God, some have been and continue to be against the Will of God.

The gospel has led the alcoholic to give up drinking, the drug addict to drop their trade, and provides the path for eternal life. Lives and marriages are restored. It was God and the Bible that was the foundation that pulled me and my wife away from a broken, failed marriage into a strong, prosperous, loving, and powerful marriage and provided a strong foundation to raise our children. There are really two primary ways to find God's will and direction, and that is through prayer and the Bible. It is the Bible and the gospel that provides answers for life, not your Compromised Church. People need a strong foundation, not modern pop psychology sprinkled with a few Bible verses. "For the word of God is quick, and powerful, and sharper than any two edged sword, piercing even to the dividing asunder of soul and spirit."[108] "It is treason to men's souls to conceal the plain truth of salvation beneath a cloud of words."[109]

You can walk around the Compromised Churches of today and see the broken people, broken families, and broken children. There is no power of God changing lives, because some reside in a place where there is no God. The Compromised Churches have missed their real purpose. Instead of strong doctrine, strong sermon, and strong families, you get strong plays, strong ideas, and fancy talk. Bibles are no longer carried around, read, or a part of lives. It is no longer a foundation to build upon, but a book to pull quotes from. All of this can be justified by the works still being done, the money still flowing in, the programs being produced, and the occasional success story. The foundation that is crumbling during this dance with apostasy is just another unnecessary causality of war from the Compromised Church. The country club church is fun for a period, but it does not produce true disciples, just shattered lives, shattered families, shattered dreams, and shattered purposes.

---

[108] Heb. 4:12 (KJV).
[109] Spurgeon, Charles. "Be Plain" *The Sword and the Trowel*, January, 1865.

IV. Große Übel kamen aus der Kirche

Out of the East, across the ocean, a strong leader was starting to grip the nation and put his mark on it. His personal rapid rise to power paralleled his nation's rise from a defeated nation, to a nation restored to its former greatness. In just four years he took an economy that was so collapsed, it took wheelbarrows full of deflated dollars to buy a loaf of bread, to a restored and vibrant economy. He provided vacations and nationalized health care along with school training, controlled crime, and undertook great public works programs. He most importantly took a nation defeated by the first World War and restored hope and glory to the people. His oratorical accomplishments were so legendary that women would swoon at the sound of his voice and some would collapse at his speeches, as he held the audience in his rapt attention. Winston Churchill noted in 1937 that his accomplishments were "Among the most remarkable in the whole history of the world."[110] By the time he had complete control of the nation at the height of his power, some thought that he was only part man, the other part divine.

Today's parents have a plethora of names to call their boys that begin with the letter A such as Andy, Aaron, and Alexander, but no one picks Adolf. Historians have noted that only if Adolf Hitler had died before

---

[110] Lutzer, Erwin W., and Eric Metaxas. *When a Nation Forgets God 7 Lessons We Must Learn from Nazi Germany*. Chicago: Moody Publishers, 2016, 46.

World War II he could have gone down as "Adolf the Great."[111] But this did not happen, and history does not recognize a great Adolf, but rather a delusional homicidal maniac. Did he change from a great leader to a homicidal maniac, or was the homicidal maniac able to play the part of a great leader? The people of Germany were eager and desperate to pledge their loyalty to someone who would save their finances and their pride. They found that person and pledged their unconditional loyalty to him, prior to learning the conditions. A History book can tell you that "History repeats itself" and to study History to "Discover the Past, Understand the Present, and Master the Future." The Bible tells us that another leader will come and save the world from its economic distress, captivate millions with miracles and supernatural power, similar to but on a much larger scale than Hitler did. The Bible refers to him as the AntiChrist, and will lead millions to an even greater destruction.

Approximately 98% of Germany was affiliated with the church when Hitler came to power. Now, that is a deceiving statistic as almost all children were baptized from birth into the Church and most people never bothered to leave the church, even though the church played no part in many lives. However, there still was a strong undercurrent of faith for many, and the Church was a part of the people, part of the lives, part of that culture. Prior to Hitler's arrival, theological liberalism had set the stage and invaded the Church. The congregants would decide which parts of the Bible were true and which were not, different ideas were explored, and the philosophers and scientists took precedence over Biblical truth, weakening the faith of large groups of people. For many, Christianity was a religion, maintaining its status as part of the culture, but it was not a life-changing faith. It was this culture that Hitler was able to begin his work with.

---

[111] Ibid., 47.

Hitler's beliefs seem to be more complex on the surface prior to diving into his character. He loved the atheistic philosopher Friedrick Nietzsche, dragged around Arthur Schopenhauer's five volume set during the war, and seemed to be also influenced by Immauel Kant and Hegel. Hitler was steeped in Darwinian philosophies, black magic and the satanic arts. Hitler was such a fan of Nietzche and Darwin that he passed out copies of their works to associates, such as Mussolini, when he met him in Italy.

Hitler's hatred and murder of the Jews is well known. But Hitler didn't limit his wrath towards the Jews. He was an equal opportunity murderer, with a secondary focus on all of what he saw as the inferior races including the gypsies, jews, blacks, metally challenged, homosexuals, those with birth defects, etc. Hitler believed the weaker races should not be allowed to breed with stronger races which would not establish an evolutionary higher state of being. Hitler saw the German people as the superior race designed to rule the world, with the Jews, Gypsies, and blacks at the bottom. "The evolutionary philosophies espoused by Charles Darwin were at the core of Hitler's ideology, and this belief in the superiority of the Aryan race motivated the Third Reich to implement the practices of eugenics, euthanasia, forced sterilization, and racial extermination."[112] Hitler was intent on speeding up the natural evolutionary process to create what he saw as the master Aryan race by the forced elimination of all non-desirable races. When the persecution started, brown triangles identified gypsies, purple triangles identified non-conforming Christian groups, black triangles identified vagrants, and pink triangles for homosexuals and pedophiles. If any humor can be found from this time period, it might be found in the 1936 Olympics held in Berlin, Germany. A delusional Hitler took his band of "superior" athletes to the games that he was hosting to prove racial superiority. Hitler was

---

[112] Comfort, Ray. *Hitler, God and the Bible*. Washington: WND Books, 2012, 100.

enraged beyond reason when the star of the show turned out to be a black American athlete, Jesse Owens, who destroyed his German competition right in front of Adolf Hitler, in his hometown. Jesse Owens won 4 gold medals and set a world record, which due to the politically charged nature of the event, could be considered one of the greatest performances in athletic history.

    Darwin seems to have left a deep impression on Hitler. Darwin's 1859 *The Origin of Species* was originally titled "*On the Origin of Species by Means of Natural Selection, or the Preservation of Favoured Races in the Struggle for Life.*" In his next book, *The Descent of Man* (1871), Darwin ranked races in terms of what he believed was their nearness and likeness to gorillas. He then went on to propose the extermination of races he scientifically defined as inferior. If this were not done, he claimed, those races with their higher birth rates would exhaust the resources needed for the survival of the superior races, dragging down all civilization. Darwin argued that advanced societies should not waste time and money on the mentally ill or those with birth defects. He saw these unfit members of our species as ones that ought not to survive. Similar to the days of Antiquity when babies that were born that seemed to be genetically inferior in size would be abandoned in the wilderness. And while "Darwinism by itself did not produce the Holocaust, but without Darwinism, especially in its social Darwinist and eugenics permutations, neither Hitler nor his Nazi followers would have had the necessary scientific underpinnings to convince themselves and their collaborators that one of the world's greatest atrocities was really morally praiseworthy. Darwinism—or at least some naturalistic interpretations of Darwinism—succeeded in turning morality on its head"[113] The German intellectuals, social reformers, physicians, and scientists of the late 19th and early 20th century were enraptured with the Darwinian new way of thinking,

---

[113] Weikart, Richard. *From Darwin to Hitler: Evolutionary Ethics, Eugenics and Racism in Germany.* Basingstoke: Palgrave Macmillan, 2006, 233.

including embracing the moral implications that derived from it. Hitler saw black Africans as "healthy, though primitive and inferior, human beings."[114]

Most Christians are naive and think the devil is a cartoon character with pointy ears and a pitchfork. "For we wrestle not against flesh and blood, but against principalities, against powers, against the rulers of the darkness of this world, against spiritual wickedness in high places."[115] The fact is, while most of the population stays in some sort of Agnosticism fumbling between the worlds, there are a few that have grasped a hold of the power of God. Likewise, there are many books, accounts, and stories, of those who have intentionally grasped a hold of Luciferian power. Hitler may have been one of those men. Embracing many occult practices while mocking a few of them, he had a love for Black Magic and some of the Satanic Arts. He may have received more than he bargained for. Rauschning describes a recurring scenario: "He yells for help ... seized with power that makes him tremble so violently his bed shakes ... in his bedroom he is muttering ... 'It is he! It is he! He's here!' His lips turn blue ... He was dripping with sweat ... He was given a massage and something to drink ... Then all of a sudden he screamed, 'There! Over there in the corner!'"[116] While Hitler may have experienced a greater depth of evil and gone further into this movement, this was not limited to Adolf Hitler. "Heinrich Himmler's masseur said that the nation was caught up in 'the mysticism of a political movement' and in 'no country were so many miracles performed, so many ghosts conjured, so many illnesses cured by magnetism, so many horoscopes read.' There were telepathy, seances,

---

[114] Weikart, Richard. *Hitler's Religion: the Twisted Beliefs That Drove the Third Reich*. Washington, DC: Regnery History, 2016, **90**.
[115] **Eph. 6:12 (KJV)**
[116] Lutzer, Erwin W. *Hitlers Cross: How the Cross Was Used to Promote the Nazi Agenda*. Chicago: Moody Publishers, 2016, **85**.

and spiritual experiences of every sort, which camouflaged Hitler's deceptions."[117]

Hitler had obvious influences from the demonic realm along with those of secular and atheistic philosophers. But Christianity was the religion Hitler claimed to be a part of. Hitler was raised in a Catholic school and made numerous references to Christianity in his speeches, often referring to himself as God's agent raised up to save Germany and destroy the Jews. On April 12, 1922, he stated: "My Christian feeling directs me to my Lord and Savior as a fighter . . . As a Christian I do not have the duty to allow the wool to be pulled over my eyes, but I have the duty to be a fighter for the truth and for what is right . . . As a Christian I also have a duty toward my own people."[118] In 1936, after coming to power, he stated: "Let us fall down upon our knees and beg the Almighty to grant us the strength to prevail in the struggle for freedom and the future and the honor and the peace of our Volk, so help us God!"[119] Since no politician in the history of humankind has ever told a lie, and apparently the only barrier to being a Christian is to go to a Catholic school and mention Christianity in some speeches, this is proof positive for some that Adolf was a Christian.

But there are some problems underneath the surface. Hitler's Catholic teacher allegedly told his parents in front of him that young Adolf was a lost soul in which there was no hope. Little Adolf responded by telling his teacher that "Some scholars doubt there is an afterlife."[120] Otto Strasser, a leader in the early Nazi movement prior to breaking away told his brother: "We are Christians; without Christianity Europe is lost. Hitler is an atheist"[121] In a 1933 speech, Hitler stated: "The unity of the Germans

---
[117] Ibid., 84.
[118] Weikart, Richard. *Hitler's Religion: the Twisted Beliefs That Drove the Third Reich*. Washington, DC: Regnery History, 2016, 1.
[119] Ibid., x.
[120] Ibid., 41.
[121] Ibid., xi.

must be guaranteed by a new worldview, since Christianity in its present form is no longer equal to the demands being placed on the bearers of national unity."[122] Joseph Goebbels stated in his diary that "The Fuhrer is deeply religious, but entirely anti-Christian. He sees in Christianity a symptom of decay. Rightly so it is a strat deposited by the Jewish race."[123] Goebbels confirmed that Hitler was able to camouflage his religious position to placate the masses and not only wanted to withdraw from the Catholic Church but to "Wage war against it."[124] The Nazi regime created "The Nazi Master Plan: the Persecution of the Christian Churches," which detailed Hitler's idea to take control of the churches as "An integral part of the National Socialist scheme of world conquest."[125] Hitler saw that "In the German Reich—and according to our view, everyone can be saved in his own fashion!"[126] Hitler confessed to Hans Ziegler that: "You must know, I am a heathen. I understand that to mean: a non-Christian. Of course I have an inward relationship to a cosmic Almighty, to a Godhead."[127] Hitler believed there was something else, but scoffed at all Christian essential doctrines such as the Fall, the Virgin Birth, redemption from sin through Jesus Christ and the Bible which caused "Mental disorders and delusions."[128] Hitler stated: "Christianity is the most insane thing that a human brain in its delusion has ever brought forth, a mockery of everything divine."[129] Hitler's final religious wish for his faith was eventually fulfilled when he stated in 1942 that "He did not want any priests within ten kilometers of his funeral."[130] There were no priests

---

[122] Ibid., xxi.
[123] Ibid., 2.
[124] Ibid., 7.
[125] Comfort, Ray. *Hitler, God and the Bible*. Washington: WND Books, 2012, **130**.
[126] Weikart, Richard. *Hitler's Religion: the Twisted Beliefs That Drove the Third Reich*. Washington, DC: Regnery History, 2016, **9**.
[127] ibid., 92.
[128] ibid., 103.
[129] Ibid., 976.
[130] Ibid., 89.

around Hitler's bunker in April of 1945, when Hitler drank cyanide, prior to shooting himself in the head.

Regardless of Hitler's personal faith, his strongest influence was felt on the church. Hitler loved the church, as long as he could control and manipulate the church, which he did. Hitler coined the term: "Positive Christianity" to reflect his views. Positive Christianity eliminated sin, salvation, and Christ's death and resurrection and replaced it with some of the "Positive" aspects of Christianity that Hitler enjoyed. He twisted History and the truth around as he saw fit. Hitler eliminated the entire Old Testament as he saw it as a "Jewish Book" and saw Jesus as a German that fought and was eventually killed by the Jews. This is an obvious error as, while the Old Testament might be a Jewish book, so is the New Testament and Jesus was Jewish, likely without the blue eyes you see in some paintings, and the Bible refers to the Jewish race as "God's chosen people." Hitler hated the "weak" or "soft" parts of Christianity that dealt with sin and forgiveness and wanted to rewrite Christianity as a German force, with Hitler as its leader, to vanquish its opposition. A Christianity not of meekness, but that of a sword. In Mein Kampf, Hitler presented Jesus as a whip-bearing savior sent to stand against the Jews who eventually killed him. He saw the Jews as destroying the racial basis of the Germanic existence.

So Adolf Hitler loved the churches and allowed them to thrive and flourish, underneath his rules and his command. Many pastors tried to compromise and, torn between God and Caesar, they tried to serve both. They preached, taught, and sang hymns with swastikas still hanging in their churches. If the gospel was occasionally preached it would only be done with a Nazified purpose, such as resentment towards the Jewish race with a push to be a good German nationalist. Hitler propped himself up as the head of the church and incorporated his own writings and ideologies into the church in place of Christ's. The *Thirty-Point Program*

For The National Reich Church stated the church was established absolutely and exclusively in the service of but one doctrine: race and nation. The Bible and other Christian publications would not be imported into Germany. The National Reich Church made it its duty to use all of its energy to popularize *Mein Kampf*; all of the altars had *Mein Kampf*, the most sacred book to the German nation and God. To the left of the altar would be a sword, and all crucifixes must be cleared away to make way for the swastika. A few Biblical verses from the Bible were hand-picked to reinforce the reign of terror such as Romans 13:1-2 about being in subjection to the governing authorities. Evil was called good and good was called evil. And most importantly: "The National Reich Church does not acknowledge forgiveness of sins. It represents the standpoint which it will always proclaim that a sin once committed will be ruthlessly punished by the honorable and indestructible laws of nature and punishment will follow during the sinner's lifetime."[131]

The German Christian movement rose up alongside Hitler's "Positive Christianity" and rooted itself into the Protestant movement. The leaders of the German Christain churches established the "Institute for Research into and Elimination of Jewish Influence in German Church Life." Its aim was a "new reception of the unadulterated Gospel by the people of the Third Reich."[132] They published their own catechism called *Deutsche mit Gott* or *Germans with God* and their own version of the New Testament called *The Message of God*. This paraphrased fragmented version of the Bible portrayed Jesus as a non Jew whose life purpose was not atonement, but fighting against the Jewish race which eventually killed him. The entire Old Testament was eliminated, and it contained 60% fewer words than the original New Testament. Jesus was portrayed as a human warrior fighting the evil of his day. The Sabbath was changed

---

[131] Comfort, Ray. *Hitler, God and the Bible.* Washington: WND Books, 2012, **120-124.**
[132] "Complicity in the Holocaust." Resistance!? Protestant Christians under the Nazi Regime. Accessed February 10, 2020. https://en.evangelischer-widerstand.de/html/view.php?type=dokument&id=76.

to holiday, and the Sermon on the Mount eliminated any blessing for the merciful, among other changes. 12 new commandments replaced the original ten:

1. Honor God and believe in him wholeheartedly.
2. Seek out the peace of God.
3. Avoid all hypocrisy.
4. Holy is your health and life.
5. Holy is your well-being and honor.
6. Holy is your truth and fidelity.
7. Honor your father and mother—your children are your aid and example.
8. Keep the blood pure and the marriage holy.
9. Maintain and multiply the heritage of your forefathers.
10. Be ready to help and forgive.
11. Honor your Fuhrer and master.
12. Joyously serve the people with work and sacrifice.[133]

While controlling the church was of essential importance to Hitler, he really needed more than the church, he needed to control everything. This is how a mediocre artist was able to seize complete control of a nation. Schools, Institutions, Businesses, and the Government were taken over. This man solidified the nation behind him along with his unwavering followers before he started sharing his more controversial views, views that previously never would have been accepted. This was after all the land of truth and reason, the land of Luther. So Hitler restored economic greatness and provided hope, then he was able to gain control. The Bible tells us this will happen again, probably in a similar way, with more devastating results. First Hitler attacked the previous holidays such as Christmas and Easter, which he eliminated, creating new holidays on

---

[133] Grigg, Russell. "Choose Country." Creation.com | Creation Ministries International. Accessed February 10, 2020. https://creation.com/hitler-bible.

different dates. Gun control laws and regulations were implemented, to prevent hunting accidents. State identification cards were issued, and citizens were forced to carry them at all times. Freedom of speech was then limited. Individual liberties were sacrificed for the good of the country. Businesses became entwined with more rules and regulation, and people had less control over their individual lives.

Hitler controlled the entire system and used lying as his means of control. It is how he killed 11 million people through institutionalized killing, 6 million which were Jews and 5 million other undesirables, not counting the nearly 34 million Germans and Europeans that died as a result of his war. Hitler would starve the Jewish children and call it: "A low calorie diet." He convinced Jews to willingly load themselves on trains to Auschwitz "For their protection and safety." One key to Adolf Hitler's success was telling large lies instead of the small ones. In Mein Kampf he stated: "All this was inspired by the principle—which is quite true in itself—that in the big lie there is always a certain force of credibility: because the broad masses of a nation are always more easily corrupted in the deeper strata of their emotional nature than consciously or voluntarily: and thus in the primitive simplicity of their minds they more readily fall victims to the big lie than the small lie, since they themselves often tell small lies in little matters but would be ashamed to resort to large-scale falsehoods."[134] Today Christians in America have a choice between Republicans and Democrats when they head to the ballet box. I think that sometimes, the correct choice in voting, regardless of the candidate or party, is the one that leads to less government.

Out of the ashes of evil, greatness did rise. Dietrich Bonhoeffer, Niemoller, and others fought the evil regime, and in many cases it cost them their lives. Bonhoeffer said that "When God calls a man, he bids him come and die" which he wrote and then was killed for standing in the way

---

[134] Hitler, Adolf. *Mein Kampf.* Stone Mountain, Georgia: White Wolf, 2014, **104.**

of Hitler and his Nazi church. As the majority of the churches, pastors, Christians, schools, general population and the governmental institutions threw their complete and unconditional support behind Hitler's regime, there were a few pastors and people that risked and oftentimes lost their lives in opposition. Some historians lamented that if only the opposition was a little stronger, Hitler could have been stopped. But many were content to conform and compromise:

> I lived in Germany during the Nazi Holocaust. I considered myself a Christian. We heard stories of what was happening to the Jews, but we tried to distance ourselves from it, because, what could anyone do to stop it? A railroad track ran behind our small church and each Sunday morning we could hear the whistle in the distance and then the wheels coming over the tracks. We became disturbed when we heard the cries coming from the train as it passed by. We realized that it was carrying Jews like cattle in the cars! Week after week the whistle would blow. We dreaded to hear the sound of those wheels because we knew that we would hear the cries of the Jews en route to a death camp. Their screams tormented us. We knew the time the train was coming and when we heard the whistle blow we began singing hymns. By the time the train came past our church we were singing at the top of our voices. If we heard the screams, we sang more loudly and soon we heard them no more. Years have passed and no one talks about it anymore. But I still hear that train whistle in my sleep. God forgive me; forgive all of us who called ourselves Christians yet did nothing to intervene.[135]

Today there are no Hitlers or World Wars. The Jewish people and other "undesirables" are not shipped off to camps. It is a different time period and culture, and technology has changed. But there are some similarities. The Nazi Church which practiced "Positive Christianity" eliminated foundational doctrines such as sin, salvation, and Christ's

---

[135] Lutzer, Erwin W., and Eric Metaxas. *When a Nation Forgets God 7 Lessons We Must Learn from Nazi Germany*. Chicago: Moody Publishers, 2016, **25-26.**

death and resurrection. Today the Compromised Church movement eliminates foundational doctrines such as sin, salvation, and Christ's death and resurrection. The nazified church used Positive Christianity and put the Fuhrer as the head of the church to unconditionally rule it. Today, across many churches, the pastor serves as Fuhrer and rules over his subjects with absolute control and dominion. As the nazified church watched when the Jews were being sent to concentration camps or burned alive, our churches today watch as our sheep are slowly getting wounded and tortured as souls are getting slaughtered. In Nazi Germany, people could turn a blind eye and tell themselves it was okay when a Jewish businessman had his storefront burned down or had his children taken away, they could compromise, they still went to church, they still did religious activities, they would sing songs in church, they could still call themselves Christians, many went to church once per week, as they did before. Today in Compromised Churches across America, people come to church on occasion to sing songs, drink coffee, socialize; religion helps them feel better about themselves as they turn a blind eye to the plea for help from the world, and that from their own church.

When Adolf Hitler was coming to power, 98% of Germany was associated with the church. While Hitler could mock Christianity off the record, on the record, he had to occasionally use religious terminology to gain the trust of the people. Hitler was opportunistic, he used religion for his glory and that of Germany. Today, pastors at Compromised Churches are opportunistic; they use religion for wealth creation and for their glory, and that of their church. In many cases, they have replaced Christ as the head of the church. One of the first things Hitler did when creating his "Positive Christianity" movement was to eliminate traditional Christian doctrine that has been used throughout history, such as sin and the atonement, so he could present his new writings, and head in a new direction. Today in Compromised Churches across America, traditional historical Christian doctrine may be put up on the church's websites, but it will not be found in the churches, as their true doctrine is determined by Hollywood and cultural standards. Gone is the idea of using the Bible as a source of truth; new writings and a new direction point to self-help and self-improvement. Each man strives for the glory of himself, over that of his neighbor, as does the world and that of Nazi Germany. Adolf Hitler preferred Mein Kampf to the Bible and the swastika to the cross; today the dollar takes precedence to the cross and self-interest takes priority to the Bible. Lies, deception, and distortion replace theology and doctrine. Satan can do more damage by using the church, being friends with the church, manipulating the truths of the Church, than he can do without it. All it takes is a few key compromises. What is important to remember is that Hitler did not set out to destroy the church. He loved the church and wanted to use it for his glory and purpose; all it would take is a few key compromises. Today pastors try to create a message of substance and conform with modern culture and, at the same time, they open their Bibles to search for truth while the swastika of compromise is dangling from their necks.

> "And so I believe today that my conduct is in accordance with the will of the Almighty Creator. In standing guard against the Jew I am defending the handiwork of the Lord." Adolf Hitler - Mein Kampf

V. Control in the Church

> For the word of God is quick, and powerful, and sharper than any twoedged sword, piercing even to the dividing asunder of soul and spirit, and of the joints and marrow, and is a discerner of the thoughts and intents of the heart.[136]

It is this piercing of the heart that has terrified certain oppressive nations that went to great lengths to prevent this book from penetrating their borders. If the Bible has the power to change hearts, minds, and souls, then it has the power to change nations, so it must be kept hidden, diluted, and diffused. Kept in a box outside of the common man. Numerous communist and dictatorship type countries have kept control of their reign of terror by keeping the Bible, a beacon of freedom, outside of their borders. The Catholic church was able to form into a Catholic empire with the power to control men, income, souls, wage war, and dictate foreign policy and control countries by keeping the Bible away from the common man. World War II gave us the trifecta of death with Hitler, Stalin, and Mussolini. Like his friend Hitler, Mussolini originally hated the church before deciding to use it for his purposes, also instituting the same governmental control and persecution of the Jews.

Stalin just took a completely different approach with his USSR anti-religious campaign and atheistic push which banned the Bible and killed vast quantities of people. Stalin also had a more unique killing method

---

[136] Heb. 4:12 (KJV)

than Hitler. If Stalin was really mad at someone, he made sure to kill that person, the entire family, the entire neighborhood of that person, all of his friends and associates, and random people that came in contact with this person. Stalin had a significantly higher kill count than Hitler, but was also an American ally, so he gets a partial pass in History under the guise "An enemy of your enemy is your friend." Idi Amin liked to peel people's skin off and feed it to them while torturing them to death. Pol Pot just killed large groups of people without the theatrics, both oppressive societies relying on control that banned the truth of God's light. Today, top vacation destinations such as North Korea, Somalia, Morocco, and Libya all have Bible-free oppressive regimes. China is looking to sinicize Christianity, or change Christianity in China, by "retranslating" the Old Testament by filling it with socialist ideals and Chinese culture with additional new commentary in the New Testament, to make Chinese culture more divine.[137] Sometimes it is easier to alter the contents of the Bible rather than just eliminating it. By creating a new powerless book and allowing people to pass it out as much as they like, they can keep the same amount of control and deception.

Now of course not all Atheistic or Secular countries or leaders turn into blood-soaking murderers. They can be great leaders and run a nice country. There is as much danger in a Theocracy as Communism. History has shown us that the more control the government of a country has, the less freedom the people have. Some governments exist for the people to thrive, others exist for the people to serve them. Likewise, some churches exist for the people to thrive, other churches exist for the people to serve them.

Control can be the lifeblood of many churches. Many churches use various methods of control to keep income up or retain the image of the

---

[137] "China Trying to 'Rewrite the Bible,' Force Churches to Sing Communist Anthems." The Christian Post. Accessed February 10, 2020. http://www.christianpost.com/news/china-trying-to-rewrite-the-bible-force-churches-sing-communist-anthems.html.

pastor. Twisting and hiding the truth is the vexillum operandi or standard operation for all of the groups that rely on distortions of truth instead of truth. Depending on the extent of this control, these groups can be called cults. There are a few types. You have the cult portrayed by Hollywood, where everyone drinks poison and chants weird things. Then you have the theological cult, when the pastor's words take precedence over the Word of God. And then you have the control cult, when the pastor uses religion to control the people in order to retain power for himself. A cult may not necessarily look like something out of a Hollywood movie, it may just look like your church.

Jehovah's Witnesses live dedicated and pure lives and are notorious for going door to door to spread their faith. And in all fairness, going door to door probably does create more converts to the cause than the seeker technique of Netflixing something from the couch. They actively live out their faith, which is something that should be commended. But if you gauge it against the Bible and traditional Christianity, it is distorted. They do not believe that Jesus has any divinity, but rather see him as a creation of God. True worship must belong to Jehovah's alone and not the trinity, and there is no eternal separation from God at the end of our lives. The founder of the religion, Charles Taze Russell, "Once declared that it would be better to leave the Scriptures unread and read his books rather than to read the Scriptures and neglect his books."[138] Jehovah's Witnesses rely primarily on their distorted watchtower tracks as their primary path to truth. They also have their own version of the Bible, the New World Translation of the Bible or NWT. This translation of the Bible was interestingly enough created with "No known translators with recognized degrees in Greek or Hebrew exegesis or translation."[139] Rather, it appears to have tampered the original scriptures to twist them to align themselves

---

[138] Martin, Walter, and Ravi K. Zacharias. *The Kingdom of the Cults*. Minneapolis, MN: Bethany House Publishers, 2003, **57**.
[139] Ibid., 93.

with the beliefs of the Jehovah's Witnesses.

The Witnesses rely on the Watchtower magazines and their version of the Bible and stay away from other Christian publications and versions of correctly translated Bibles. If you talk with a Jehovah's Witness, they will insist that their church is just one of the many denominations in the body of Christ and they are interchangeable. If you tell them that you are already a Christian, they will just nod their head and stay on your doorstep. The reality is that they do not want to lead you to Christ, but lead you towards their religion. A religion they themselves are trapped in. If they question the teachings and authority of their own church, they are excluded from membership. One misplaced question can turn former friends and brothers into strangers and outsiders. "A disfellowshipped person is cut off from the congregation, and the congregation has nothing to do with him. Those in the congregation will not extend the hand of fellowship to this one, nor will they so much as say 'hello' or 'good-bye' to him..."[140] Absolute control and the exclusion of those with different opinions is how they survive. They glean converts from the Christian community. "The Watchtower leadership sensed that within the midst of Christendom were millions of professing Christians who were not well grounded in 'the truths once delivered to the saints,' and who would rather easily be pried loose from the churches and led into a new and revitalized Watchtower organization. The Society calculated, and that rightly, that this lack of proper knowledge of God and the widespread acceptance of half-truths in Christendom would yield vast masses of men and women, if the whole matter were wisely attacked, the attack sustained and the results contained, and then reused in an ever-widening circle."[141]

Mormons make up another large group in America. They are some of the nicest people in America and live moral lives. While RVing through

---

[140] ibid., 67.
[141] Ibid., 147.

Utah, a beautiful Morman repeatedly insisted that I use his truck and stay at his house as I did not have a truck or place to stay. I had a hard time convincing him that my RV served as not only a mode of transportation but also as a place to stay as it had a shower, fridge, and beds in it. Mormons stay away from alcohol, tobacco, and even caffeine and of course have a heavy reliance on tithing. This is a billion dollar industry. They are great people, but their doctrine is different. They believe that eternal life in the celestial heavens must be earned through good works, humankind is the same species as God, and that the Trinity is three separate gods born in different times and places. They also believe the Earth is one of several inhabited planets ruled over by gods and goddesses who were at one time humans. The Mormon church has a President and the appointed quorum of twelve Apostles that get direct revelation from God and then give it to the common man. There is structure and control in place. The President and Apostles set the rules, hear from God, then give it to the church goers, as they can not hear from God themselves. Mormons are given *The Book of Mormon*, as a sacred text along with *Doctrine and Covenants*, and *The Pearl of Great Price*. The Mormons do acknowledge the actual Bible, but use a heavily cross-referenced version of it. *The Book of Mormon* holds authority over it. The Bible has two testaments and the Mormons see the *Book of Morman* as just another testament of Jesus Christ, a third testament. The Mormons know that as long as they keep their people in their building, under their leaders, and heavily indoctrinated in their teachings and writings, that pulling verses out of a heavily footnoted Bible is not going to hurt anything, but rather establish authority and help them align with traditional Christianity.

Christian Science was started by Mary Baker Eddy, who claimed to have been healed from a life-threatening disease through prayer. Christian Scientists believe that sickness is an illusion that can be handled by prayer only. And there is some truth to some of that. Prayer and a walk in the fresh air, maybe a dose of garlic and Vitamin C is going to do more for your body if you have a cold, than heading to a doctor where you will probably just pick up the flu. And prayer can heal other physical attacks that are more than just psychosomatic or mild issues. I met a man who just swam a mile in the ocean, originally diagnosed with an aggressive form of cancer with one month to live. He attributed prayer and faith as his answer, and one year after his diagnosis of death, he is still taking life one month at a time. God can and does heal. Likewise, doctors can and do heal and can get you some good antibodies. The problem with Christian Science is you do not need to rely on the teachings of Mary Baker Eddy and be under their doctrines and their sets of rules, you can access God and healing on your own. The Bible also calls us towards prayer and fasting and prayer and supplication, which is an intense and earnest cry out to the Creator. Like all distortions of Christianity, Christian Scientists alter the truth and deny that Jesus is God and believe that sin, death, and evil do not exist, and rely on their own writings instead of the Word of God.

Unitarian Universalists are actually a merger of Unitarians and Universalists. They started with a Christian heritage, they value all faith religions, and believe all religions lead to God. They reject the Bible as the infallible word of God and many do not believe in God at all, though they do see it as a source of culture and wisdom. Rev. David McFarland summarizes it well: "The Bible is holy scripture because it is the living document and foundation of many important faiths, including Unitarian Universalism. To abandon the Bible would mean alienation from one of the world's most important influences on religious thought—liberal and otherwise. Our UU Principles and Purposes are saturated with biblical concepts and ideals. Our concept of respect for the web of existence, for instance, emanates from a stream of thought that flows through the Psalms and the Prophets from that same God of Genesis who declared the goodness of creation."[142] So they basically respect the Bible, understand that it has an important role in History and other faiths, and pick out pieces of it that they like. They of course reject the concept of sin and Christ's atonement of sin. They preach love, acceptance and tolerance. While their religious roots are Judeo-Christian, today's Unitarian Universalists encompass a large spectrum of faith perspectives including: Atheist/Agnostic, Buddhist, Christian, Hindu, Humanist, Jewish, Muslim, Pagan, and more.[143] The first Unitarian Universalist church of Ann Arbor's website states the "Senior ministers' warm and engaging preaching style appeals to both heart and head. He is a deeply thoughtful person with a multicultural background, drawing inspiration from Uism, Hinduism, Buddhism, Humanism, Christianity and Lakota spirituality."[144] They sing songs such as: "There is more love somewhere" and "Praise the source of faith and learning" and read secular sections of books on their Sundays. They do not bother to distort the Bible or create their own version of it. They have a Sunday service called a church, ministers, and some Christian phrases, but are more of a secular humanist organization involved in humanitarian good works projects and the intentional merger of all religions under the banner of love. In a way, they are just a more advanced version of their compatriots in the Compromised Churches, they are just a little bit more honest with themselves.

The final group to be mentioned is the Seventh Day Adventists. The recent movie *Hacksaw Ridge* featured a war hero that saved 74 lives during the Battle of Okinawa. This man did it without touching a gun, which he refused to do, and saved lives under heavy artillery. He was a Seventh Day Adventist named Desmond Doss, whose life was portrayed in

---

[142] "Unitarian Universalist Views of the Bible." UUA.org, February 27, 2017. https://www.uua.org/beliefs/what-we-believe/sacred-texts/bible.
[143] Administrator. "What UUs Believe." What UUs Believe. Accessed February 10, 2020. https://uuaa.org/index.php/about-us/unitarian-universalism/what-uus-believe.
[144] "Our Ministers and Staff." Ministers and Staff. Accessed February 10, 2020. https://uuaa.org/index.php/about-us/ministers-and-staff.

the movie along with the persecution he encountered for his beliefs. The movie was historically accurate; the only thing Mel Gibson changed was at the end of the movie when Doss was placed on a stretcher. "In real life, Doss had another wounded man take his place on the stretcher. After treating the soldier, a sniper shot fractured Doss' arm and he crawled 300 yards (270 m) to safety after being left alone for five hours. Gibson omitted this from the film because he felt that the audience would not find the scene believable."[145] Apparently this man's real life story was too dramatic for Hollywood.

Seventh Day Adventists honor the Sabbath on Saturday, believe in pre-tribulation, eat healthy and stay away from alcohol and other drugs, and live to honor God. Studies have shown they live an average of 10 years longer than the average Christian due to their healthy eating habits. The official stance is the Bible is the word of God. Many Seventh Day Churches present traditional Biblical teachings and offer powerfully Biblically based messages. In many places, Seventh Day Churches are great churches filled with great people. However, contrary to official church policy, some churches will put the teachings of Ellen White over to or equal to that of the Bible. While Desmond Doss may be a new hero of the movement, Ellen White is the founder whose writings are enriched heavily in the church, and in some cases, take precedence over the Bible. Some Seventh Day Adventists say Ellen White is just as inspired as Isaiah or one of God's other prophets. The Clear Word Bible, a paraphrase written by an Adventist, where major portions of the translation are material added by the author,[146] is picking up popularity in some Adventist circles.

There are numerous alternative versions of Christianity that proliferate across America. Today many churches are blurring the lines between truth and untruth, between traditional Christianity and the

---

[145] "Hacksaw Ridge." Wikipedia. Wikimedia Foundation, February 10, 2020. https://en.wikipedia.org/wiki/Hacksaw_Ridge.
[146] "The Clear Word." Wikipedia. Wikimedia Foundation, January 27, 2020. https://en.wikipedia.org/wiki/The_Clear_Word.

opinions of their leader. A religious cult, or unhealthy church if you prefer that term, is an organization that has departed mainstream Christianity to establish doctrines that are not Biblical. They hold the leaders' contradictions and the leaders opinions over the Word of God. Biblical doctrine is slightly twisted over time until it becomes so different that it blurs the lines between truth and untruth. The roots generally lie in man's desire for control and place their authority above that of God's authority.

The definition of what actually constitutes a cult and if something is just "Cult like" is difficult to define. Forcing various groups into a box and calling them a cult is not the point. What is the point, is that various groups use control and manipulation to keep people in bondage to the institution. Any time you take someone's opinion, whether you consider that person to be a prophet, pastor, or elder, and put their word above God's word, you have a problem. And any time you take another book and put that book equal to or above God's word, you have a problem.

I have had an opportunity to witness deception in the church first hand. Years ago, I had a fractured marriage. My response to the real estate and financial collapse that occurred was to work more to solve the problems. My wife's response to my response was to join a small church under the guise that they would be able to evangelize the world. The only evangelization the pastor ever did was preach his gospel of wealth and self enrichment. Apparently making money eclipsed actual evangelization. I would attend sometimes and enjoyed some messages and believed parts of it, but never got fully immersed as I was battling the bondages of agnosticism and selfishnessism, and just did not completely conform to their little group. Sometimes I saw it as something that kept my wife occupied while I could do what I wanted. I really didn't realize how bad things were until my wife took the pastor's advice, drained our bank account to give it to him, and left me and took our only son.

It was then, broken in mind and spirit, financially devastated, and just lost my wife and only son, that I cried out to a God that I wasn't even really sure existed. I wept out what was a lifetime of frustrations and pain. It was there, to my surprise, that I heard the voice of God. I picked up the Bible and started reading: "In the beginning God created the heavens and the earth." The words started washing over my partially agnostic mind. As I kept reading, I learned about fasting, prayer, honoring God, and righteousness. My mind and actions started changing. It was God that raised me up and showed me how to be a father, it was God that raised me up and showed me how to be a husband, and it was God that raised me up and showed me how to be a businessman. My marriage was not only restored but became a vibrant marriage, my only son was restored and God provided multiple sons and beautiful daughters. I would read and meditate on verses over and over again such as "Blessed is the man who trusts in the Lord, And whose hope is the Lord. For he shall be like a tree planted by the waters, Which spreads out its roots by the river, And will not fear when heat comes; But its leaf will be green, And will not be anxious in the year of drought, Nor will cease from yielding fruit."[147] I learned that faith may be a gift, but like everything else in life it could be developed. I devoured apologetic books, scripture, and eradicated the abundant bondages and sin in my life. I started changing decisions, which changed my life. I stopped working seven days a week to spend time with my family and honored a day set aside for God.

Upon leaving the church, my wife was terrified something bad was going to happen to her, because that is what the pastor told her would happen to the deserters. She lived in fear and bondage for the next year, and it really took even longer to get some of the lies out of her head. But in the midst of deceptive pastors and people, lies and manipulation, tricks and trickery, God was there to guide our family down a new path, towards a new life. There would be trials and difficulties, as can be expected in

---

[147] Jer. 17:7-8 (NKJV)

life, but this time we were not alone; it was God that was walking with us, guiding our family through the process and towards his truth.

> The church has always faced the temptation to modify the gospel or make it secondary to a given political, philosophical, or cultural agenda ... What is different today is that the message of the cross is being ignored even by those who claim to be saved by its message. At the very time when the gospel must be proclaimed most clearly we are hearing muffled voices even from some of the great evangelical pulpits of our land.[148]

> "We cannot stay silent as the blade of death runs through God's church" - Erwin Lutzer

---

[148] Lutzer, Erwin W., and Eric Metaxas. *When a Nation Forgets God 7 Lessons We Must Learn from Nazi Germany*. Chicago: Moody Publishers, 2016, 139-140.

VI. Twisting Truth

"If you wish to know God, you must know his Word. If you wish to perceive his power, you must see how he works by his Word. If you wish to know his purpose before it comes to pass, you can only discover it by his Word." –Charles Spurgeon

John 8:31 "If you abide in my word, you are truly my disciples."

Just because something has the word Bible on it, does not mean that it contains the power of God's truth. The Golf Bible is not a real Bible. Anton Lavay's Satanic Bible is not good devotional material. Adolf Hitler and the Nazis did not do a good job on God's word. I am not holding my breath on Communist China's remake of the Bible with Buddhism and Confucianism embedded in it. Thomas Jefferson cut and pasted the supernatural events out of the Bible he didn't agree with to create the Jeffersonian Bible. Jehovah's Witnesses have the New World Translation, Mormons have their book of Mormon, Christian Science has the writings of Mary Baker Eddy, Unitarian Universalists have their secular humanist writings, The New Age Movement has the Aquarian Gospel of Jesus Christ, the Seventh Day Adventists have the Clear Word Bible, and those of the New Apostolic Reformation have their Passion Translation.

Distorting scriptures to structure your point of view is not something new. It has been done before. "There are some things in them that are hard to understand, which the ignorant and unstable twist to their own destruction, as they do the other Scriptures."[149] What is new, at least in American church history, is having those distortions and influences penetrate mainstream Christianity. It has been common that while in church, pastors will sprinkle in a few Bible verses to add authority to their point. But now the sources themselves being used are being watered down. Paraphrased multiple versions of the Bible are generally used not to establish the authority of the Bible, but to establish the authority of whatever point the Pastor is trying to make.

One paraphrased Bible that was gaining traction is Eugene Peterson's The Message paraphrase. And the problem is not Eugene himself; many of his writings are pretty good, and it can be interesting to read the Bible from another perspective or watch *The Bible*, a great movie produced by Roma Downey and Mark Burnett. This movie was paraphrased; it was not word for word. The problem was not the act of paraphrasing the book, as it could be used for recreational reading, as one could read other writings from Eugene. The problem is using it as a source of Biblical authority in messages and as a primary study Bible. This was a concern that Eugene Peterson himself had. Eugene Peterson, the author of the Message paraphrase, as reported in Christianity Today (December 23, 2002), stated when asked if he considered The Message God's Word: "In a congregation where somebody uses it in the Scripture reading, it makes me uneasy. I would never recommend it to be used as, 'Hear the Word of God from the Message.' It surprises me how many do. I like to hear those more formal languages in the pulpit. I did the Beatitudes in about 10 minutes."

The problem with using the Message paraphrase as a source of Biblical authority is that, in many cases, it says the exact opposite of what the real Bible says. In other cases, it muddies the original meaning. There

---

[149] 2 Peter 3:16b (ESV)

are thousands of examples. One is the Lord's Prayer which starts off with: "Our Father in heaven, Reveal who you are. Set the world right; Do what's best—as above, so below." Matthew 6:9-10 MSG. Contrast that to the original in the KJV: "Our Father which art in heaven, Hallowed be thy name. Thy kingdom come. Thy will be done in earth, as it is in heaven." Colossians 2:9 NIV says: "For in Him all the fullness of Deity dwells in bodily form, and in Him you have been made complete, and He is the head over all rule and authority." Very clear and easy to understand. The Message says: "Everything of God gets expressed in him, so you can see and hear him clearly. You don't need a telescope, a microscope, or a horoscope to realize the fullness of Christ." None of the Greek texts imply using a horoscope to realize the fullness of Christ, and actually this is specifically banned earlier in the book.

Romans 15:13 says basically the same thing in all of the translations, from the KJV: Now the God of hope fill you with all joy and peace in believing, that ye may abound in hope, through the power of the Holy Ghost. The Message states: Oh! May the God of green hope fill you up with joy, fill you up with peace, so that your believing lives, filled with the life-giving energy of the Holy Spirit, will brim over with hope! Note that there is no "God of green hope" in any of the Greek manuscripts nor do they mention life-giving energy of the Holy Spirit. We now have a new commandment listed in scriptures, remember that the next time you check out with a plastic bag at the grocery store.

1 Corinthians 6:9-10 KJV states: "Know ye not that the unrighteous shall not inherit the kingdom of God? Be not deceived: neither fornicators, nor idolaters, nor adulterers, nor effeminate, nor abusers of themselves with mankind, Nor thieves, nor covetous, nor drunkards, nor revilers, nor extortioners, shall inherit the kingdom of God." The Message states: "Don't you realize that this is not the way to live? Unjust people who don't care about God will not be joining in his kingdom. Those who

use and abuse each other, use and abuse sex, use and abuse the earth and everything in it, don't qualify as citizens in God's kingdom." Again we see the role of environmentalism being listed as a new sin in God's commandments.

Romans 8:35 in the KJV says: "Who shall separate us from the love of Christ? shall tribulation, or distress, or persecution, or famine, or nakedness, or peril, or sword?" The ESV says "Who shall separate us from the love of Christ? Shall tribulation, or distress, or persecution, or famine, or nakedness, or danger, or sword? The NASB says essentially the same thing and the NIV says: "Who shall separate us from the love of Christ? Shall trouble or hardship or persecution or famine or nakedness or danger or sword?" Even most paraphrases fall in line such as the GNT. Contrast this to the Message which states: "Do you think anyone is going to be able to drive a wedge between us and Christ's love for us? There is no way! Not trouble, not hard times, not hatred, not hunger, not homelessness, not bullying threats, not backstabbing, not even the worst sins listed in Scripture." The last part of this verse introduces a new theological element that was not there before.

The American Banking Association used to have a two-week training camp in which they would send hundreds of bank tellers to Washington in order to detect counterfeit money. They would not show them any counterfeit money; they only allowed real money to pass through their hands, by feeling, touching, and seeing the real thing, they would know a counterfeit when they see it.[150] People need to get a real Bible in their hands to avoid the deception from those that were sent to help them. People need to see the truth for themselves.

The Bible is the power of God that has the opportunity to change lives, but by keeping this from the people, it keeps them in bondage and cannot set the people free. "This Book of the Law shall not depart from

---

[150] Martin, Walter, and Ravi K. Zacharias. *The Kingdom of the Cults*. Minneapolis, MN: Bethany House Publishers, 2003, **23.**

your mouth, but you shall meditate in it day and night, that you may observe to do according to all that is written in it. For then you will make your way prosperous, and then you will have good success."[151] This is how the Catholic church used to keep people under the bondage of the Catholic Empire; they used Latin Bibles for the German-speaking people, while the Bible was kept away from the people. "I will delight myself in your statutes; I will not forget your word." Either all of the versions of the Bible are wrong, including the old original manuscripts, or the Message Bible is wrong. It is one or the other. You can not alter the Word of God, and still consider it the Word of God. All Scripture is God-breathed and is useful for teaching, rebuking, correcting and training in righteousness"[152]

We have to make sure the book is changing the culture, not changing the book to conform to the culture. Everyone has preconceived ideas and opinions, which is why most Bible versions such as the KJV, NRSV, ASV, NKJV, or ESV were translated using some of the greatest pastors, theologians, and scholars available. The ESV was composed with over 100 of the leading scholars and pastors. The King James version composed by 47 of the greatest scholars of the time. Most Bible versions were composed with a board of people. The problem when you are not relying on a group of people, but relying on one person, preconceived opinions or ideas can intentionally or unintentionally alter what God originally intended to say. Dr. Larry Spargimino stated: "The Message is a prime example of how a particular Bible version is being used to weaken churches and to allow false and dangerous doctrines to be accepted by the masses of undiscerning church members."[153]

Keeping the Word of God accurate is important, Revelations states: "For I testify unto every man that heareth the words of the prophecy of this book, If any man shall add unto these things, God shall add unto him

---

[151] Josh. 1:8 (NKJV)
[152] 2 Tim. 3:16 (NIV)
[153] Dr. Noah Hutchings, *The Dark Side of the Purpose Driven Church The dark side of the Purpose Driven Church* (Crane: Defender Publication, 2011), 71.

the plagues that were written in this book." [154] This prophecy may be pertaining to the book of Revelation, yet if: "Man shall not live on bread alone, but on every word that comes from the mouth of God."[155] And: "The words of the Lord are pure words: as silver tried in a furnace of earth, purified seven times."[156] Then how can man change the meaning of the words to match their views? We also have warnings listed here: "Every word of God proves true; he is a shield to those who take refuge in him. Do not add to his words, lest he rebuke you and you be found a liar."[157] And: "You shall not add to the word that I command you, nor take from it, that you may keep the commandments of the Lord your God that I command you."[158]

On one hand you have something which could provide new insight in some areas and could be enjoyable as a recreational read, and this may not be a problem. On the other hand, a lot of people in these types of churches are not reading any version of the Bible, let alone reading multiple versions and comparing them to the Greek, Hebrew, and Aramaic for historical accuracy. They are relying on this source as their primary Bible. As sheep heading to the slaughter, they trust pastors and leadership to guide them in the right direction. "An upright shepherd and minister must improve his flock by edification, and also resist and defend it; otherwise, if resisting be absent, the wolf devours the sheep."[159] The paraphrases have some good in them as the Compromised Churches have some good in them, but they are able to slightly mask truth, water down the power of God's word just enough to render it ineffective. And the main problem with the paraphrases isn't the current paraphrases, it is the copy of the copied paraphrase that will come out in the future. As they

---

[154] Rev. 22:18 (KJV)
[155] Matt. 4:4 (NIV)
[156] Ps. 12:6 (KJV)
[157] Prov. 30:5-6 (ESV)
[158] Deut. 4:2 (ESV)
[159] Martin Luther, *The Table Talk of Martin Luther*, trans by William Hazlitt, (London: H.G. Bohn, 1857), 183.

continue to push paraphrases in different directions, man can create whatever meaning he intends with them, and that is the real point. It is not the paraphrases themselves, it is the idea that man's word can trump God's word. "You therefore, beloved, knowing this beforehand, be on your guard so that you are not carried away by the error of unprincipled men and fall from your own steadfastness."[160]

Without a written standard of righteousness, a source of truth, established standards, we are entering a wild west arena with an 'anything goes' morality. One church hired a psychic medium on staff for their church.[161] Some churches have beer on tap to make them more user friendly.[162] Lying from the pulpit is commonplace and distorting doctrine is to be expected. Prosperity preachers pimp their congregation for riches and fame. "Who supposes that godliness is a means of gain."[163] Other groups hide the truth to promote themselves and their institutions through self-help and entertainment. "Woe to those who call evil good and good evil."[164] Pastors are rising themselves up for their own glory, their own institutions, across America. And this is not limited to America. A Pastor in Ghana had his congregants drink his dirty bathwater to receive some type of healing because God told him to.[165] The fabric of the Bible has been ingrained into American culture and the church. As that is being removed, we are falling into a free-for-all morality. The wolves are getting well fed at the expense of the sheep.

Rome had a large influence on structuring America at its

---

[160] NASB 2 Pet. 3:16-17
[161] "The Vision Church of Atlanta GA Now Has A Psychic Medium On Staff!!" The Old Black Church. Accessed February 11, 2020. https://theoldblackchurch.blogspot.com/2019/05/the-vision-church-of-atlanta-ga-now-has.html.
[162] Wolinski, Cat, and Greater Purpose Community Church / Facebook.com. "California Church Serves Beer During Services, Will Open Brewery." VinePair. Accessed March 10, 2020. https://vinepair.com/booze-news/california-church-serves-beer-will-open-brewery/.
[163] 1 Tim. 6:5b (NASB)
[164] Isa. 5:20 (ESV)
[165] "Ghanaian Pastor Bathes in Church, Tells Congregation to Drink Bathwater for 'Anointing.'" Disrn. Accessed February 11, 2020. https://disrn.com/news/ghanaians-pastor-bathes-in-church-tells-congregation-to-drink-bathwater-for-anointing.

conception. Fortunately, Rome did not influence the morality of America upon its conception. America was founded on Biblical values. The founders were mostly Christian with strong Biblical beliefs, the ones that were deists or agnostics, still studied the Bible.[166] In a ten-year study undertaken at the University of Houston, researchers examined 15,000 documents from America's founders and determined that 34% of their quotations came from the Bible, the highest by far of any source.[167] Hundreds of ideas from Bible verses can be found in the Constitution, Declaration, some of the original Amendments to the Constitution, the Mayflower compact, the blue laws forcing businesses to be closed on Sunday, etc. As we can see the results in the American society as it slides away from truth, so can we see the results in the American church, as some slide into Apostasy.

All Bible versions can be divided into three categories: The first type are going to be the literal translations also known as formal equivalent. This is what it says, a direct literal word-for-word translation from the original text. While you can always debate over a Greek word or two, and find a possible better meaning or eliminate a grammatical error, these translations are going to be the most accurate as they take a literal reading of the Bible. You have the KJV, NASB, RSV, NKJV, ASV, RSV, YLT, RYLT, and JPS versions that are considered literal translations. The next group are the thought-for-thought translations; they took the thoughts, meanings, and intentions of the Bible and reworded them into modern English, also known as dynamic equivalent. These would be the CEV, REB, NJB, NAB, ESV*, NIV, and NEB. The ESV has a star next to it because it is an "essentially literal translation"; it basically belongs in the first group, it didn't quite make it, it is between the groups. The third group are

---

[166] Books have been written about the historical sources of the faith of our fathers, such as George Washington crediting "divine providence" on the creation of America, it would take another chapter or book to properly give credit, so it will be omitted here.
[167] "Faith Facts." The Bible and Government - Faith Facts. Accessed February 11, 2020. http://www.faithfacts.org/christ-and-the-culture/the-bible-and-government.

paraphrases. These take the Word of God and paraphrase them into the authors meanings, thoughts, and ideas. Some examples would be The Message Bible, The Living Bible, and the Good News Bible.

Another interesting thing on Bible versions is the text they came from. The New Testament was composed mostly of letters to churches or historical accounts, some of which only had numerous fragments to deal with. Erasmus was the first to put these scrap pieces together; he gave us a Greek New Testament, and the Textus Receptus or Received Text comes from this work. English translations were then created from Erasmus, including Tyndale's, the Geneva Bible, and the KJV Bible. Luther also used it, but Wycliffe translated directly from the Latin Vulgate. The NKJV and Young's Literal Translation and NYLT also translated from this text. Then a pair of people called B.F. Wescott and F.J.A. Hort translated from a new group of documents and gave us the critical text. Most of the recent Bibles come from the work of Wescott and Hort. There is some debate as to which group of Greek documents are superior.

Translations are tough, because you are taking one word from one language where another word in a different language may not exist. Just look at a thesaurus and see how many variations of the same word we have in the English language. Finding the exact best word can be challenging. Languages change, as you can see just from Old English to our modern English. Luther had to attack the "papal bulls and donkeys" who tried to nitpick his version. It is amazing how accurate the Bible is, considering how many times it was translated, and compared to other writings from antiquity. The Dead Sea Scrolls found in 1947 show how accurate the scribes were, and many of them considered this their "Life's work."

You can find a word or two that can be translated better in other versions of the Bible or run into a few translation issues. The ESV omits entire verses such as Matthew 17:21 which highlights the importance of prayer and fasting. The Textus Receptus and many other original Greek texts such as those found in Codex W, D, E, L, do have this verse. However, it is important to note that there are a few original documents that do not have this verse, either due to scribal error or accidental omission. Some believe that some of the scribes could have unintentionally added it, as fasting was so closely linked to prayer that they may have assumed it was part of the process. It seems as if the NASB version of the Bible did better in this regard, as they bracket the verse and footnote that some early versions do not contain this verse.[168] Picking the right word from one language to the next can be more of a difficult task than it seems, as sometimes there are not direct words that correspond. But the concern isn't about a word or two that could have possibly been translated better, but it is a concern when you have thousands of translation issues.

The King James version says that Jonah was swallowed by a whale, which has led to many Jonah and the Whale children's stories. Maybe he was and he miraculously survived, which is possible, but some see this as problematic due to the digestive juices found in whales. In the book of Jonah, we have the Hebrew word Dag Gadol, which is commonly interpreted to mean great fish. However, in Matthew the writer uses the Greek word Ketos, which could mean great or large aquatic animal, sea monster, fish, or whale. The NASB selected the term Sea Monster, while the ESV picked great fish. So while it is possible it was a whale, it could have been a wide variety of items from the sea that swallowed Jonah, possibly one that is currently extinct. The creator of the heavens and the universe that formed everything certainly has the capability to create and appoint something from his sea to handle Jonah.

This book is not going to make an attempt or a declaration of what the best version of the Bible is, as the breadth of study would be too large.

---

[168] Wayne, Luke. "Christian Apologetics & Research Ministry." CARM.org, February 27, 2019. https://carm.org/KJVO/was-matthew-17-21-removed-from-modern-bibles.

It is a good question, just not answered here. In this book, the KJV version was used the most, along with a dose of ESV, a sprinkling of NKJV, a drop of NIV for nostalgia, and a dot of YLT, NASB, and ASV. Picking one version of a good translation of the Bible for primary study is essential to avoid deception while remaining free to read other versions. While some people may be able to read through multiple versions and note and compare the versions and research some of the greek words, your average church-going member only gets a dose of confusion with a dozen Bible versions.

The KJV is a beautiful literary accurate translation with a Shakespearean flow to it. However, an argument can be made that the 1611 version of KJV or the West Saxon Gospels is better than this version. NASB seems to be a great translation and might be the most literal and easily readable today as the scholars goal was to adhere to the original languages as close as possible, but wouldn't Luther's German Bible or the Old English Hexateuch be better? The RSV is great, but reading the Greek, Hebrew, and Aramaic could be better. ESV is a great translation composed by over 100 of the leading scholars and pastors, but you could always read the Dead Sea Scrolls or something. The ASV is an accurate translation, but Tyndale's English version of the Bible could always be read for greater accuracy with a bonus touch of historical flair and linguistic enhancement. As a historical side note, William Tyndale was burned at the stake by the Catholic Church for creating this first English version.

I might be able to say my favorite version of the Bible is superior to your favorite version, as I think my Ford truck is superior to your Chevy truck. But another Chevy truck fan can rave about their vehicle that they were able to put 300,000 miles on it and it still is running great. Today we have the choice of many great and good translations as you may have a choice of many good and great truck options. But you wouldn't want to buy a truck without an engine or tires, as you would not want to rely on a Bible that has been altered and is devoid of the power of God. **The Bible** has always been reinterpreted by people to fit their needs, and now the actual words are being changed to fit their agendas. For those with doubts, or those who are battling the bondages of agnosticism, a strong foundation on God's word is needed, and apologetics can help. If the foundation is compromised or non-existent, it is only a matter of time. If the Bible truly is God's word to man, it can not be altered. Eugene Peterson stated: "We don't twist God's word to suit ourselves."[169] The Good News version of the Bible, one of the first paraphrases, came around to provide a more readable version and to tinker around with the text in an attempt to get it right. In his radio address in response to this, former president Ronald Reagan stated: "It will not dawn on them that it has already been gotten right."

Philippians 1:17b: "Knowing that I am set for the defence of the gospel."

Romans 1:16: "For I am not ashamed of the gospel of Christ: for it is the power of God unto salvation to every one that believeth; to the Jew first and also to the Greek.

---

[169] 2 Cor. 4: 1-2 (Msg)

VII. History Repeats Itself

The Bible gives us a clear path, a precise guide, from Adam to the Cross, to the Glory of God, and to Eternity. On a map, it would look like a highway connecting major cities. But if you look at actual Christian History, it is nothing like this. If you charted Christian History on a graph, it wouldn't look like a highway connecting major cities, but more like a spiderweb, filled with constant dead ends, heading sideways, at angles, wrong directions, and oftentimes backwards. The path of Christian history is filled with mistakes, errors, and misdirections. The right path, the path towards the Glory of God and the Cross of Christ, was always there, it was always able to be followed, oftentimes it just wasn't. Oftentimes God's people have decided to wander in the thickets or just completely head in the opposite direction.

A primary portion of the Old Testament is Christian History. We have Samuel, Kings, Chronicles, Joshua, Ezra, Nehemiah, amongst others. And when you look at the history, you quickly notice patterns continually repeated throughout the books. God's people and the nation of Israel generally fall into sin and bondage, chase after false idols, God judges them and shakes them up, they repent or someone comes to lead them towards God, things get fixed, then the cycle repeats itself. We had Noah, who "walked with God,"[170] a lone righteous man amongst a violent and corrupt Earth who refused to repent. We have Moses, who saved God's people from slavery, they then built an idol because he was taking too long on the mountain, and Moses then ground up this idol and made the people drink it. We have Eli, whose two sons "were sons of Belial; they knew not the Lord."[171] 2 Corinthians 6:15 presents Belial as Satan, while other accounts have Belial as a top Demon, the Demon of lies, a source of great evil. Regardless, we have God's priests in God's temple serving Satan. They stole the meat that was supposed to be used for God's sacrifices, instead using it for personal gain, threatening those that would not conform.

We have Gideon standing against the false teachings and idolatry of his day, attacking Baal and freeing God's people. We have Micah, from mount Ephraim, who lived when "Every man did that which was right in his own eyes."[172] Micah made his own temple with false gods and made his sons the priests, later paying a Levite, a true priest of God, to be a priest in his temple. Micah had slidden so far into apostasy, he thought he would receive God's blessing for what he did, instead of his wrath. After the period of Judges, we have the period of the Kings, starting with Saul.

Samuel restored righteousness to Israel, then Saul became the first king of Israel, who started off as a great king, then allowed small compromises, which resulted in: "You have rejected the word of the LORD, and the LORD has rejected you from being king over Israel."[173] And, "The Lord repented that he had made Saul king over Israel."[174] The next king, David, was a man after His own heart."[175] A great king, that ruled over a great kingdom, but did allow a few compromises that brought afflictions

---

[170] Gen 6:9b (KJV)
[171] 2 Kings 2:12b (KJV)
[172] Judges 17:6b (KJV)
[173] 1 Sam. 15:26b (NASB)
[174] 1 Sam 15:35b (KJV)
[175] 1 Sam. 13:14b (NASB)

into his life. His son Solomon brought Israel into the height of her glory, but Solomon chased after other things and other gods, more compromises. So God took this great kingdom from him, tore it into pieces, and his son Rehoboam was left with a divided kingdom to rule, that would get progressively weaker as they continued to stray from the truth.

By 648 B.C., there is not much left of the formerly great nation of Israel. It is a divided kingdom, the north sacked by Assyria, the two tribes that make up Judah just hanging on. Josiah is the king of Judah. The book of the law is found during temple renovations, and read to the King. When the king hears the words, he tears his clothes, and weeps, to hear how far his people have fallen. Josiah institutes immediate reforms, repents, and destroys the false idols. He made a covenant to walk after the Lord, keep his commandments, and eradicate the sinful practices of Judah. Because of this, the prophetess Huldah tells Josiah he will be taken early, to miss the devastation that will come. That devastation comes in the wrath of the Babylonian empire, which takes Judah in 586 B.C. Babylon takes many Jews from Judah and puts them in exile or holds them as prisoners to serve the king. Daniel is one of them. Babylon is now the global empire of the day, with the Jews as its hostages. While Belshazzar, King of Babylon, is partying with the holy vessels from the temple, he sees the writing on the wall, Mene, Mene, Tekel, Upharsin, "Thy kingdom is divided, and given to the Medes and Persians."[176] And that is what happened; Herodotus tells us that Cyrus, King of Persia diverted the mighty Euphrates river which flowed under the gates of Babylon, marched right into the city through the now dried-up riverbed, surprising Babylon while they were busy with their feast.

Cyrus, the king of Persia, now has control of these exiled Jews. He allows Nehemiah to leave Persian control and lead the restoration efforts

---

[176] Dan. 5:28b (KJV)

of rebuilding Jerusalem's walls. This leads to "The Great Revival under Ezra," found in Nehemiah 8:1-10:39, also detailed in Ezra chapter 10 as Ezra/Nehemiah was originally one book. Ezra, who generally gets left out of the limelight, brings the book of the law of Moses, which is what they have as the Bible at that time, and brings it before the congregation and reads, before the men and women. "For all the people wept, when they heard the words of the law."[177] The people read the Bible, confessed their sins, worshipped, and repented. Many people think of a great evangelical outreach upon hearing the term revival, but really hearts need to be changed and revived prior to the evangelical outreach. The term revival is confined to believers. It refers to believers in a poor spiritual state who were brought back to vitality and power or "To recover life and vigor".[178]

Christian History through the Old Testament shows us the cycles God's people continuously repeated from faith to apostasy, to rebellion, to correction, back to faith. But it also shows us something far greater than that. Every book in the Old Testament points to the gospel. Isaiah 53:5-6 tells us:

> But He was pierced through for our transgressions, He was crushed for our iniquities; The chastening for our well-being fell upon Him, And by His scourging we are healed. All of us like sheep have gone astray, Each of us has turned to his own way; But the LORD has caused the iniquity of us all To fall on Him.[179]

The laws of the Old Testament don't really change. Jesus just added a new element to them. Previously you couldn't literally kill someone, and Jesus kept that but added that you can't even hate them. Adultery was banned in the Old Testament; that is kept, but Jesus added lusting with the eyes. While the cross crumbled some legalities, it brought into focus

---

[177] Neh. 8:9 (KJV)
[178] Dr. J Vernon Mcgee, *Thru the Bible with J. Vernon Mcgee Vol. 2* (Through the Bible Radio, 1982), page 535.
[179] Isaiah 53:5-6 (NASB)

many realities—it didn't crack the foundation but enhanced it, as now there would only be one way to enter, and that would be through the cross.

The birth of Jesus Christ is the dividing point of history. Everything before his birth is labeled B.C. or Before Christ, and everything after his birth is noted as A.D. or Anno Domini, the Year of our Lord. Some modern historians now use C.E. or B.C.E. as common era and before common era to get away from this, but the dates are still the same, as 400 B.C. and 400 B.C.E. still measure 400 years before the birth of Christ. Dionysius Exiguus, a monk who was the first to date history by the life of Christ, may have been a year or two off on his calculations, but regardless, the historical measuring stick still stands. On one aspect, the birth of Jesus surprised the Jews; they were expecting a warrior king, not a humble servant. He surprised them even more by constantly making fun of them and disrupting their religious systems.

The reason the New Testament starts off with Matthew is that Matthew provides a detailed lineage of the genealogy of Jesus Christ, including Abraham, Isaac, Jacob, the root of Jesse, and David to fulfill some of the 55 old testament prophecies concerning Christ's birth. The purpose of Jesus's arrival was not to toss some witty comments at the religious folks, or to take down the Roman establishment, but for salvation. The name Jesus is a Greek form of Hebrew Jehoshua, meaning Jehovah is salvation. The atonement of Christ is not a new idea, but one that permeates the New Testament and Christian History. In fact, 102 verses mention it. Here are a few:

> John 3:16: "For God so loved the world, that He gave His only begotten Son, that whoever believes in Him shall not perish, but have eternal life.
>
> John 1:29: "The next day he saw Jesus coming to him and said, "Behold, the Lamb of God who takes away the sin of the world!"

> Matthew 1:21: "She will bear a Son; and you shall call His name Jesus, for He will save His people from their sins."
>
> Matthew 26:28: "For this is My blood of the covenant, which is poured out for many for forgiveness of sins."
>
> 1 Corinthians 4:3-4 "Christ died for our sins according to the scriptures; And that he was buried, and that he rose again the third day."

While the purpose of God sending his only begotten son to this world for the forgiveness of our sins was the point of the visit, Christianity shook the foundations of the Roman Empire and the known world. It tore and continues to tear the fabric of society and culture. Rome saw women as property to be literally used; a wealthy roman man would have one woman for occasional pleasure sex, a young girl to satisfy daily sexual needs, and a wife to keep the house in order and maybe used as a back-up sexual object if needed. Paul's letter to Timothy opposed this culture by telling us: "Husbands, love your wives, as Christ loved the church and gave himself up for her,"[180] Slavery was prevalent during this time period and part of the culture. Paul stood against this culture, by defending a slave named Onesimus, and referring to him not as property, but as a "Brother in Christ." While we never do know if Philemon released his slave, Ignatius gives us a clue that he did, as he notes a letter written to a church leader named "Bishop Onesimus," about 50 years later.

While the Bible is the only source as the Word of God, numerous historical writers detailed this time period, such as Josephus, Suetonius, Eusebius, Philo, Clement, Tertullian, and Hegesippus. In his book *The Twelve Caesars*, Suetonius tells us about a man named Nero, a man that used to spend his evenings in disguise so he could take out his chariot to run over random people, if he wasn't using Christians as human torches to light his evening festivities. He was responsible for the deaths of Peter and Paul along with numerous other Christians. Eusebius tells us that: "Once

---

[180] Ephesians 5:25 (ESV)

Nero's power was firmly established, he plunged into nefarious vices and took up arms against the God of the universe."[181] The Bible tells us of the Herod that slaughtered babies in his attempt to kill the Christ. But History adds the tagline of "The Great" to him due to his impressive architectural accomplishments such as a subterranean sewer system. But Jospehus gives us a firsthand account into his personal life. Herod was madly in love with his wife, then went "mad" and killed her. He also killed his own sons, his brother-in-law, numerous other people, and would beat his own head when angry, not normal behavior. The Romans were men of power, wealth, control, domination, and they got that way by ruthlessly crushing their enemies and all opposition. There were no excuses, just destruction and devastation. If their infant boys were not born big enough, or if they happened to be girls, they would be left on the rocks for the sea to sweep away or food for the birds. The Bible stood in stark contrast to that of Rome, as it advocated helping the poor, the disadvantaged and widows. It was the polar opposite of the Romans that killed for power and control, and also for entertainment.

The wheels and machinery of the Roman government continued to crank and grind on as they chewed up any opposition, and they saw the new Christian movement as opposition. Jesus is killed as recorded in the gospels. According to *Foxe's Book of Martyrs*, Philip is crucified, Matthew is slain with a halberd, James referred here as James the Great is martyred, his accuser that turned James in repents and resolved "That James should not receive the crown of martyrdom alone."[182] The other James gets referred to as "James the Less," who gets beaten and stoned and, for a bonus, has his "brains dashed with a fuller's club."[183] Matthias is

---

[181] Eusebius, and Paul L. Maier. *Eusebius--the Church History*. Grand Rapids, MI: Kregel Publications, 2007, 74.
[182] Foxe, John, and William Byron Forbush. *Foxe's Book of Martyrs: a History of the Lives, Sufferings and Triumphant Deaths of the Early Christian and the Protestant Martyrs*. Milton Keynes, UK: Lightning Source UK Ltd., 2010, 2.
[183] Ibid., 2.

stoned and beheaded, Andrew is crucified on a cross, Mark is dragged to pieces, Peter is crucified upside down as he considers himself unworthy to be crucified in the same manner as Christ. Paul gets his head cut off, Jude is crucified, Bartholmew gets beaten to near death, then they get impatient and crucify him. Thomas is speared, Luke hanged, Simon crucified, and Barnabas martyred. John gets tossed in boiling oil but miraculously survives so he can be exiled to Patmos to write the book of Revelations. "And yet, notwithstanding all these continual persecutions and horrible punishments, the Church daily increased, deeply rooted in the doctrine of the apostles and of men apostolic, and watered plenteously with the blood of saints."[184]

After the death of the disciples and those of the early church, persecution continued, as it continues in parts of the globe today. Polycarp and Ignatius, influential leaders and church fathers who wrote many non-canonical influential writings were both martyred along with Justin Martyr, a famous Christian philosopher and apologist. Heavy persecutions continue. To accept Christ during this time period meant that you would continue in the suffrage that he faced. People did not turn to Jesus to live in an Osteenian utopia and become happy, healthy, and wealthy, but rather expected torture, financial devastation, and death. The persecutions continued through the period of Diocletian, where it may have peaked. He proclaimed his "Edict against the Christians," which permitted the destruction of Christian scriptures and places of worship. The persecution was intense and included torture. Peter Cubicularius was slow-roasted over an open fire with salt and vinegar during the great persecution.

The church withstood and encountered violent opposition since its inception. False teachings and heresy entered the church immediately. Really it never left. The warnings against false teachers compose a large

---

[184] Ibid., 4.

portion of the New Testament; they are actually mentioned in every book of the Bible outside of Philemon. "I know that after my departure fierce wolves will come in among you, not sparing the flock; and from among your own selves will arise men speaking twisted things, to draw away the disciples after them."[185] Paul is concerned for Timothy who was told to stay in Ephesus, "So that you may command certain men not to teach false doctrines any longer."[186] Matthew records: "For false messiahs and false prophets will appear and perform great signs and wonders to deceive, if possible, even the elect."[187] Peter warns us: "But false prophets also arose among the people, just as there will be false teachers among you, who will secretly bring in destructive heresies"[188]

So early Christians started placing an emphasis on theology, truth and doctrine from the beginning, to start cutting through the heresy. The Council of Jerusalem was set up in AD 50 to handle concern dealing with new Gentile Converts. Then we had the false teachings of Gnosticism and Docetism. Origen fought the Gnostics, he took a purity pledge that was so dedicated that he castrated himself. Other false teachers would come in waves. Marcion claimed the Old Testament God and the New Testament God were actually separate deities, and the supreme God of the universe was all loving and would never punish anyone. Marcion created his own version of the Bible, which only included eleven of the New Testament books, an edited version of Luke's gospel and ten of Paul's letters.[189] Faith declarations were created and powerful Christian leaders were risen to help stop the false teachings. Irenaeus was an early leading theologian of the church who wrote Adversus Haereses (Against Heresies), and Hippolytus was sent to the mines then martyred after recording the Apostolike Paradosis or "Hand on the Word of God".

---

[185] Acts 20:29-30 (ESV)
[186] 1 Timothy 1:3-7 (NIV)
[187] Matt. 24:24 (NIV)
[188] 2 Pet. 2:1a (ESV)
[189] Jones, Timothy P. *Christian History Made Easy*. Peabody: Rose Publishing, 2017, 24-25.

As heavy and intense as the persecution was, it came to an abrupt stop. The blood of the martyrs that was endured during the reign of Diocletian strengthened the cause of the Christians. Constantine brought in a new era of Christianity, that not only allowed Christianity, but made it the preferred religion. At the battle of Milvian, Constantine faced Maxentius with an army twice the size. Constantine had a new symbol on his shield, the monogram of Christ, that he placed on his shield from a day vision he saw with his troops and a dream the previous night where Christ appeared to him and said "In hoc signo vinces," meaning "By this sign you will conquer." Constantine won the battle and "Deemed himself the servant God had chosen to convert the Roman Empire to the Christian faith."[190] The ancient writer Eusebius fawned over him and referred to him as "The Emperor beloved by God."[191]

Constantine issued the Edict of Milan in 313, Legalizing Christianity less than a decade after the Great Persecution. However, while Christians were now safe from physical harm, False doctrines and bad ideas pillaged Christianity at a more intense rate. The Council of Nicea in 325 had every overseer in the Roman empire invited to deal with Arianism, an idea that Christ was not divine and subordinate to God. This council rejected Arianism and confessed the full deity of Jesus Christ and its belief in the Trinity. A creed, or declaration of faith, was established called the Nicene Creed. The First Council of Constantinople was later established in 381 to confirm the Nicene Creed and expanded doctrine to produce the Niceno-Constantinopolitan Creed. So back in the early church period, forming doctrine and creeds and fighting heresy was considered the life's work of many of these essential church leaders. The Athanasian Creed is established and the Apostles Creed is also created. First found in 390AD, it says:

---

[190] Eusebius, and Paul L. Maier. *Eusebius--the Church History*. Grand Rapids, MI: Kregel Publications, 2007, 305-306.
[191] Ibid., 333.

I believe in God, the Father almighty, creator of heaven and earth. I believe in Jesus Christ, his only Son, our Lord. He was conceived by the power of the Holy Spirit and born of the virgin Mary. He suffered under Pontius Pilate, was crucified, died, and was buried. He descended to the dead. On the third day he rose again. He ascended into heaven, and is seated at the right hand of the Father. He will come again to judge the living and the dead. I believe in the Holy Spirit, the holy catholic Church, the communion of the saints, the forgiveness of sins, the resurrection of the body, and the life everlasting. Amen.

Jerome then translated the Bible into Latin which is called the Vulgate. Then the greatest theologian of his time, possibly of all time, Augustine starts writing. In *The City of God*, Augustine shows us the two realms that exist on earth, The City of God and the City of Mankind. In *Confessions*, Augustine details his conversion and provides his confession: "Sins of self-indulgence are committed when the soul fails to govern the impulses from which it derives bodily pleasure. In the same way, if the rational mind is corrupt, mistaken ideas and false beliefs will poison life. In those days my mind was corrupt."[192] He also notes: "The world is drunk with the invisible wine of its own perverted, earthbound will."[193] Augustine's piece *On Christian Doctrine* establishes doctrinal foundations such as: "To see God, the soul must be purified."[194] and "The fulfillment and end of scripture is the Love of God and our neighbor."[195]

In the middle of the 5th century we have Patrick who became a missionary to Ireland. He used familiar Irish symbols such as the three-leafed shamrock to explain the trinity. Today we have St. Patrick's Day in honor of him, a day many get drunk to honor a devout and dedicated Christian and missionary. In 681, we had the Third Council of

---

[192] Augustine, and R. S. Pine-Coffin. *Confessions*. London: Penguin, 1961, 86.
[193] Ibid., 45.
[194] Augustine. *On Christian Doctrine*. USA: Beloved Publishing, 2014, 13.
[195] Ibid., 31.

Constantinople to discuss Monothelitism which was gaining rapid popularity prior to being denounced as heretical by this council. The Second Council of Nicaea in 787 stamped out the idea that Jesus was not God's son by nature. Alfred the Great, the English King, translates part of the Bible into English.

In the year 800 AD the church created the first emperor, Charles Augustus known as Charlemagne. Religion is getting militarized, using forced conversions and conquests. This took the church down a dangerous path, staining the cross with power, money, and blood. Religion militarized with the power of the Catholic Church. Theology and doctrine lost precedence to power, glory, and military conquests. In 1095, Pope Urban II launched his war to take Jerusalem back from the Muslims, known as the Crusades. He claimed that anyone who died fighting his war, which he claimed was God's war, would receive immediate forgiveness from God. Waves of crusades would then follow. We then had the Inquisitions, another church-mandated wave of death. In 1201, Pope Innocent III claimed power over all the secular rulers. We are now in a dark period of church history. Absolute power corrupts absolutely, which is evidenced by the Church in this time period, which tried its hardest to keep the gospel away from the common man. While the Catholic church continued into corruption, the black death or bubonic plague rolled over Europe, engulfing up to 88% of the population in Constantinople and over half the population in other areas. This nursery rhyme possibly came from this time period: *Ring around the Rosey, pocket full of posies, ashes, ashes, we all fall down!* Some say the posey was a flower you put in your pocket to help combat the stench of death. The Rosie was the first sign of the plague, a red rosie ring on your flesh. The next thing you knew, you fell with the other dead and were cremated into ashes. When the people most definitely needed the Bible and a true relationship with their God, the church offered them inquisitions, crusades, indulgences, tithes, and religious activities.

But amidst the death and apostasy, bright spots were starting to emerge. Thomas Aquinas was a great theologian that helped many people and was able to incorporate Christian theology with another popular philosopher of the time, Aristotle. Aquinas stated that: "Sacred scripture leads to this life in two ways, by commanding and by helping."[196] John Wycliffe came up with the idea that every church member should strive to understand the Bible and read it in their own language, so he started an English version of it. He was pronounced a Heretic by the church, but they did not get the chance to kill him, as he died of natural causes. Jan Hus then started to embrace the ideas of Wycliffe by saying that people should obey the church, but only if the church agreed with the Bible. They burned him alive for that comment and then dug up John Wycliffe's bones and burned them also. The Renaissance was now coming into power, with its focus on Greek art, culture, writing, and for many a renewed interest in the Greek New Testament, an interest in scripture started. Then Erasmus published a Greek New Testament edition called the Textus Receptus or Received Text and boldly said the church was wrong in some areas, using the Crusades as an example. A feisty and fiery monk was then finally able to finish what these men started, crumbling this institution of apostasy.

Luther's followers would be called Lutherans, and they would concrete Christian doctrine in various forms including the Augsburg Confession. A fire of the mind was now lit, a revolution was started, and people would be set free from religious bondage. John Calvin then came along and focused on predestination as one of his theologies. Today, if you believe in predestination, it is said that you have a Calvinistic view on things, which derives of course from John Calvin. Later on, Jacob Arminius

---

[196] McInerny, Ralph. *Thomas Aquinas: Selected Writings*. London, England. Penguin Books, 1998, 7.

was hired to defend Calvinistic doctrine. Upon researching to create his defense to support Calvinism, he came to reject the Calvinistic claims. He stated that Jesus died for everyone, but his death only redeems believers. Followers of this theological point would be called Armenians. Anabaptists introduced the separation of church and state and introduced adult baptism. Another group would originate over the issue of Baptism, and they are called Baptists today. A man named William Tyndale once got into a debate with a local priest; the priest stated that: "It would be better to be without God's law than the pope's." Tyndale responded: "If God spares my life, I will cause the plow-boy to know more about Scripture than you do."[197] He did exactly that, by translating the Greek New Testament into simple English, which cost him his life. In 1538, Pope Paul III from the Catholic church called for a reforming council to reform the Catholic Church. They acknowledged that they would give scripture and church tradition equal authority and said both faith and works were necessary for salvation.

A few hundred years later, the largest religious revival to take place was so large and intense that it changed the landscape and culture of America so greatly, that secular historians were forced to take notice. The Great Awakening started in 1730. Thousands of people came to or dedicated their lives to Christ which led to tens of thousands being saved. Entire cities were transformed, and some areas were called "Burned-over districts." After the revival came through, entire cities were changed. According to Wikipedia: "Conviction of sin was the stage that prepared someone to receive salvation, and this stage often lasted weeks or months. When under conviction, nonbelievers realized they were guilty of sin and under divine condemnation, and subsequently faced feelings of sorrow and anguish. When revivalists preached, they emphasized God's moral law to highlight the holiness of God and to spark conviction in the

---

[197] Jones, Timothy P. *Christian History Made Easy*. Peabody: Rose Publishing, 2017, **115**.

unconverted."[198] History.com tells us the major themes in this awakening were that:

> All People are born sinners
>
> All people can be saved if they confess their sins to God, seek forgiveness and accept God's grace
>
> All people can have a direct and emotional connection with God.
>
> Religion shouldn't be formal and institutionalized, but rather casual and personal.[199]

The largest religious revival to ever take place outside of the early church took the exact opposite approach of today's churches. George Whitefield is generally credited as the leader of this movement, and one account tells us that one crowd drew 23,000[200] to hear his booming voice echo across the field. People were in bushes and trees in an attempt to hear him. Whitefield's friend, Benjamin Franklin, would do calculations during some of Whitefield's speeches and estimated his voice would carry without a microphone so 30,000 people could hear it. Whitefield's largest crowd was 60,000 people in Moorfields in London, but many were turned away as they could not hear.[201] When Whitefield came to the towns, they would shut down the entire town to clamor at his speeches. George was emotional, theatrical, and had a voice that carried across the fields. Whitefield was intense in his private life, constantly studying, praying, fasting; it was said every hour of his day from early morning was accounted for. Another preacher, John Wesley, was often in the shadow of George Whitefield. But Benjamin Franklin was publishing his sermons so more people could hear the message of repentance. One sermon, entitled

---

[198] "First Great Awakening." Wikipedia. Wikimedia Foundation, February 6, 2020. https://en.wikipedia.org/wiki/First_Great_Awakening.
[199] History.com Editors. "Great Awakening." History.com. A&E Television Networks, March 7, 2018. https://www.history.com/topics/british-history/great-awakening.
[200] Tomkins, Stephen. *John Wesley: A Biography*. Grand Rapids, MI: Wm. B. Eerdmans Pub. Co., 2003, **68.**
[201] Dallimore, Arnold A. *George Whitefield: God's Anointed Servant in the Great Revival of the Eighteenth Century*. Wheaton, IL: Crossway Books, 1990, 53.

Sinners in the Hands of an Angry God, surpassed any of Whitefield's and is considered the most famous sermon ever preached on American soil. One part:

> The wrath of God is like great waters that are dammed for the present; they increase more and more, and rise higher and higher, till an outlet is given; and the longer the stream is stopped, the more rapid and mighty is its course, when once it is let loose. It is true, that judgment against your evil works has not been executed hitherto; the floods of God's vengeance have been withheld; but your guilt in the meantime is constantly increasing, and you are every day treasuring up more wrath; the waters are constantly rising, and waxing more and more mighty; and there is nothing but the mere pleasure of God, that holds the waters back, that are unwilling to be stopped, and press hard to go forward. If God should only withdraw his hand from the flood-gate, it would immediately fly open, and the fiery floods of the fierceness and wrath of God, would rush forth with inconceivable fury, and would come upon you with omnipotent power; and if your strength were ten thousand times greater than it is, yea, ten thousand times greater than the strength of the stoutest, sturdiest devil in hell, it would be nothing to withstand or endure it.

The Great Awakenings had multiple waves that would change American history. It is interesting to note that the main leaders of the greatest revivals in American history were both kicked out of the church. They were both forced to preach in the fields as most churches would not host them. Whitefield expected to be killed by the church, and since Wesley was kicked out of every church in England, he stated: "The world is my parish." In the 19th century a preacher rose up who was so powerful that he was referred to as "The Prince of Preachers" by his fellow preachers. His name was Charles Spurgeon. Like his predecessors, Spurgeon was in constant battle with the religious establishment of his day. Other evangelists would follow, such as Sojourner Truth, and Dwight

Moody. We had martyrs like Dietrich Bonhoeffer, who also became a writer, and evangelists such as Jim Elliot, who also became a martyr. Jim Elliot said before his death: "He is no fool who gives what he cannot keep to gain that which he cannot lose." The last large American Evangelist ended with Billy Graham.

Lots of important people and events were missed in this concise trip down memory lane that we call History. The study of History says that we can remember the past, understand the present, and master the future. We see that the Bible points to the Cross of Christ, from the Old Testament foundations to Christ's death on the Cross. Thousands of years of church History show us that this is the central theme of Christianity. Violence has been used against Christians since its inception, and is still used today, primarily outside of America. Tertullian stated in *Apologeticus*: "The blood of the martyrs is the seed of the church."[202] But it was deception that has been able to cause the most damage to Christianity, not violence. Christianity has seen countless attacks against the truth: Gnosticism, Sabellianism, Arianism, Pelagianism, Nestorianism, Adoptionism, Marcionism, Catharism, Gundolfo, Jansenism, amongst others. And whether we are referring to God's people as the nation of Israel, or the historical church, or the modern day church, we see the same cycles through Christian history. Periods where the church was filled with heresy, apostasy, false doctrines, and false teachings, and periods where God raised people up to fight it. From Moses, to Gideon, to Samuel, to Josiah, Daniel, Ezra, Jesus himself, the apostles, Wycliffe, Huss, Tyndale, Luther, Wesley, Whitefield, and Spurgeon. The church and God's people have continuously had to purify themselves from heresy, apostasy, false doctrines, and false teachings. At one point, the people of Israel were literally in Babylonian captivity. Today, many Christians across America are in self imposed exile, held in bondage, and are waiting to be set free.

---

[202] Tertullian, and S. Thelwall. *The Apologeticus of Tertullian*. New York: publisher not identified, 1909, Ch 50.

The history of the church, the legacy of truth, the history of God's people and what they fought and died for over thousands of years, now stands in stark contrast to that of the Compromised Churches. But the Compromised Churches are large in number, have impressive institutions, and are run by powerful and charismatic leaders with great oratorical ability. But as much as they cite themselves as examples, as much as they try to validate themselves, as much as they form a type of camaraderie with other churches, it has not always been that way. It is a new path, a new direction, one that runs with the world on a large wide-open path marching to death. But this is not the way that it has always been. The Bible has always pointed to the same message, pointed to the Cross, pointed to truth, pointed to life. The History of the Church has shown that truth has continually marched on, despite constant assaults and threats from outside and within.

Nowhere in Christian History has the central theme of Christianity been hidden to attract converts. There have been no effective Christian campaigns that hid the gospel message, in order to advance the gospel message. The message was never removed, to promote the message. Christians never contemplated coming to Jesus so that they can be a better you while they were being sawn in half. Rather, many Christians in many periods in History clearly understood the choice they were going to make; they did not come to the Cross for financial rewards or make their lives better. Rather, they expected financial devastation, persecution, and possibly torture or death. Today we have big institutions, big men with big egos, big programs, but the message that stained the ground with the blood of the apostles is missing. Prosperity teachers tell us that if we give them money, God will give you money. Faith teachers tell us that if we say the right words, we are guaranteed a great life. Seeker churches tell us the gospel message must be kept a secret, to advance the gospel. But thousands of years of Christian History shows us something different.

Christian History shows us periods of correct theology, correct doctrine, strong faith, where the world is being transformed, followed by periods of oppressiveness where the truth and the gospel are hidden. It seems to go in waves, when the light of the gospel shines the brightest, the enemy will fight the hardest. History shows us that when Christianity was shining the brightest, the people had access to the true Word of God and were not under oppressive manmade ideologies or religion. They were under God himself.

One dangerous thing that Christian History shows us is that in some cases, man has created Religion so that he can make the rules, prop himself up as some kind of leader, try to control things, and set himself in place as some type of conduit to God. In the name of Jesus, they do things contrary to the will of Jesus. History shows us that money, sex, and power have had an all too powerful theme through secular history. Unfortunately, we have seen this make its way into the Church. Christian History gives us the formula for success. After Christ's death, a handful of people spread the gospel through the entire known world at the time. They did not have Seeker Sensitive churches, Prosperity churches, participate in Friendship Evangelization, or have pastors clamoring for money. Yet they shook the foundations of the Roman Empire and changed the course of World History. Luther pierced a dagger into the religious Catholic Empire, bringing it to its knees, by bringing the truth of God's word to the people. We see powerful preachers such as Charles Spurgeon and powerful movements such as the great awakenings that followed simple formulas, giving people access to the Word of God, to truth, and preaching on sin and the need for salvation. Today's Compromised Churches are against these formulas, against truth, and against the gospel message, which makes them enemies of the Cross of Christ.

VIII. The Study of God

Theology is important. Without it, you could wander around some of the wastelands they call churches today and get confused and "Waste your life and lose your soul".[203] Theology means the study of God. Augustine's definition of theology was "Reasoning or discussion concerning the deity." Practical theology deals with God's self-revelation and activity throughout the life and ministry of human beings. Theology was once considered the topic that all gentlemen discussed, yet today it is mostly ignored. But the study or understanding of it will impact your life. If you wander around all day thinking that God hates you for some sin that you committed in the past, you will expect things to go bad in your life and they probably will. Likewise if you view God as a big bubbly clown or a giant Spongebob that loves it when you embrace sin, you will struggle in your walk. You could also have a theological view that thinks that you are saved by giving Kenneth Copeland money or by attending church, but both of these views will just waste your time and money.

God is the King of Kings over this world and rules the creation for his Glory. And that God is saviour, loves us, and sent his son Jesus Christ to atone for our sins to save us and provide eternal life. But you don't have to go back to Augustine to read Christian Theology, because J.I. Packer

---

[203] Packer, J. I. *Knowing God*. Downers Grove, IL: InterVarsity Press, 1973, **19**

has a nice easy-to-read book on the subject called *Knowing God*. J.I. Packer tells us that there is evidence of knowing God. Such as having great energy for God, great thoughts for God, great boldness for God, and great contentment in God. "Once you become aware that the main business that you are here for is to know God, most of life's problems fall into place of their own accord."[204] To know God is to have a basic understanding of him. As you know your children or know your favorite sports team, you should know God. He made us to be in a relationship with him, but you have to know someone to be in a relationship with them. You can know God through prayer, worship, and his word. Spurgeon said: "If you want to hear God, read his word, if you want to hear God out loud, read his word out loud." God is majestic, unchanging, and all powerful. Militant Atheists can raise their fists at God and declare him as dead, but this does as much good as ants on a busy New York City sidewalk protesting all the people stepping on their home. God is all powerful despite your understanding or rebellion of him. God is all wise despite what intellectual achievements you think you might have.

We have the grace of God, God regenerates sinners in Christ. By his grace we are saved. God is love. "For God so loved the world, that he gave his only begotten Son, that whosoever believeth in him should not perish, but have everlasting life.[205] His love for us covers scripture and Christain History. God is love. But if you are in a marriage and consistently cheat on your wife on a regular basis, is that truly a marriage? God is love, but if you are a parent and let your nine-year-old kid play video games and smoke pot all day long, is this truly love? God is love, but if you see a man raping a child, and do nothing, is this truly love?

God has intense love for us, but he is also our judge. He is our Father, our friend, our companion, our helper, our first love, but also our judge. We see this in the Old Testament with Sodom and Gomorrah and

---

[204] Ibid., 34.
[205] John 3:16 (KJV)

Noah. The New Testament shows us Herod, Ananias, Sapphira, and the Corinthian Church. However, not every tragedy or affliction we encounter on Earth is God's judgment; most of them are just the cycle of living in a fallen world, where rain is sent on "The just and on the unjust."[206] When the tower of Siloam fell, killing eighteen people, Jesus asked if these people thought they were the worst sinners in Jerusalem.[207] The answer was no. So afflictions and judgments are possible in this life, but don't always happen. Many carnal men have had a smile on their face till death. David laments about this in Psalms frequently. But what can be expected, is that we will all stand before his judgment one day, even Christians. "For we must all appear before the judgment seat of Christ."[208] The judge has authority, wisdom, the ability to discern truth, righteousness, and the power and authority to execute his sentence. God is a jealous God. And our actions, our decisions, our rebellion, can lead us to encounter the Wrath of God.

Today we have: "Gods of greed, pride, sex and self-will, the church mumbles on about God's kindness but says virtually nothing about his judgment."[209] The Bible makes it clear that those that defy God through every action of their life, will one day encounter the wrath of God. Revelations is filled with wrathful apocalyptic imagery; 2 Thessalonians 1:8 tells us: "In flaming fire taking vengeance on them that know not God, and that obey not the gospel of our Lord Jesus Christ."[210] Those that encounter the wrath of God are just receiving what they chose, getting what they want, the unbeliever has preferred to be by himself and eternally separated from God as they were separated from him on Earth.

> When the Son of Man comes in his glory, and all the angels with him, then he will sit on his glorious throne. Before him

---

[206] Matt. 5:45 (KJV)
[207] Luke 13:4
[208] 1 Cor. 5:10 (NIV)
[209] Packer, J. I. *Knowing God*. Downers Grove, IL: InterVarsity Press, 1973, **148.**
[210] 2 Thess. 1:8 (KJV)

will be gathered all the nations, and he will separate people one from another as a shepherd separates the sheep from the goats. And he will place the sheep on his right, but the goats on the left. Then the King will say to those on his right, 'Come, you who are blessed by my Father, inherit the kingdom prepared for you from the foundation of the world. For I was hungry and you gave me food, I was thirsty and you gave me drink, I was a stranger and you welcomed me, I was naked and you clothed me, I was sick and you visited me, I was in prison and you came to me.' [211]

But we also must remember that, "The one who will judge sinners is the very one who loved and gave his life for them. The triumphant Judge who stands at the end is none other than the dying Jesus on a cross, who has already taken the judgment of God on himself for the sake of the whole world."[212] We are dealing with a loving God, who we force to put him in a position to judge us.

We get our theology from the entire Bible, but the book of Romans is basically a book on theology and doctrine, or essential truths. This book stands against false doctrines. Romans starts out with a declarative statement: "For I am not ashamed of the gospel of Christ: for it is the power of God unto salvation to every one that believeth; to the Jew first, and also to the Greek."[213] It then tells us that: "For the wrath of God is revealed from heaven against all ungodliness and unrighteousness of men, who hold the truth in unrighteousness;"[214] It then warns about those "Who changed the truth of God into a lie."[215] Secrets and lies will one day be exposed, treachery will be brought to life, there is a standard of truth: "God shall judge the secrets of men by Jesus Christ according to the gospel."[216] While the objective is to move away from sin and towards

---

[211] Matt. 25: 31-36 (ESV)
[212] Guthrie, Shirley C. *Christian Doctrine*. Louisville, KY: Westminster John Knox Press, 2018, **388**.
[213] Rom. 1:16 (KJV)
[214] Rom. 1:18 (KJV)
[215] Rom. 1:25 (KJV)
[216] Rom. 2:16 (KJV)

righteousness, it must be acknowledged that: "All have sinned, and come short of the glory of God," and by ourselves, "There is none righteous, no, not one."[217] This verse, when combined with others, helps question the basis of the seeker movement, "There is none that seeketh after God."[218] The idea that your Christian life can be perfect through positive faith declarations is set aside by Paul telling us that we "Glory in tribulations also: knowing that tribulation worketh patience; And patience, experience; and experience, hope."[219]

But while hard challenges will be encountered in life, Paul tells us that: "I am persuaded, that neither death, nor life, nor angels, nor principalities, nor powers, nor things present, nor things to come, nor height, nor depth, nor any other creature, shall be able to separate us from the love of God, which is in Christ Jesus our Lord."[220] Sin can keep you from the heart of God. "Knowing this, that our old man is crucified with him, that the body of sin might be destroyed, that henceforth we should not serve sin. For he that is dead is freed from sin."[221] This idea is a prevalent theme in Romans which also tells us: "For sin shall not have dominion over you: for ye are not under the law, but under grace. What then? shall we sin, because we are not under the law, but under grace? God forbid."[222] The reason why is listed a little later: "For the wages of sin is death; but the gift of God is eternal life through Jesus Christ our Lord."[223] Instruction for salvation is included with: "That if thou shalt confess with thy mouth the Lord Jesus, and shalt believe in thine heart that God hath raised him from the dead, thou shalt be saved. For with the heart man believeth unto righteousness; and with the mouth confession is made unto salvation. For the scripture saith, Whosoever believeth on him

---

[217] Rom. 3:10 (KJV)
[218] Rom. 3: 11 (KJV)
[219] Rom. 5: 3-4 (KJV)
[220] Rom. 8: 38 (KJV)
[221] Rom. 6:6-7 (KJV)
[222] Rom. 6:14 (KJV)
[223] Rom. 6: 23 (KJV)

shall not be ashamed."[224] Romans concludes with a warning: "Now I beseech you, brethren, mark them which cause divisions and offences contrary to the doctrine which ye have learned; and avoid them. For they that are such serve not our Lord Jesus Christ, but their own belly; and by good works and fair speeches deceive the hearts of the simple."[225] Romans is telling us that there have been and will continue to be great speakers that deliver good speeches that sound Godly, but their primary concern is themselves.

Doctrine, goes along with Theology and comes from the Latin word "*doctrina*," meaning "teaching" or "instruction." Over the course of Christian History, we have been given doctrine, creeds, covenants, declarations, and statements of faith. Truth has been composed into declarative statements. We have the Apostles Creed, Nicene Creed, Creed of Chalcedon, The Heidelberg Catechism, Catechism of Geneva, Second Helvetic Confession, The Scots Confession, The Belgic Confession, The Gallican (or French) Confession, The Canons of the Synod of Dort, The Barmen Declaration, Westminster Standards, The Confession of 1967, The Declaration of Faith, A Brief Statement of Faith, Cuba Confession of Faith, Taiwan Confession of Faith, Korea Our confession of Faith, Japan Confession of faith, A Declaration of Faith for the Church in South Africa, the South Africa Theological Declaration, the Nashville Statement, the Statement on Social Justice and the Gospel, amongst others.

If you go too far into doctrine and theology, it can get overwhelming, possibly boring for some, and the objective of Christianity is not to be a Theologian and accumulate head knowledge, but to follow the commands of Christ. Knowledge can puff up to pride and become useless if not used for the glory of God. On the other hand, the other extreme is to ignore it. Most Compromised Churches today do not have or follow any doctrine. Whatever the world presents as good they will

---

[224] Rom. 10: 9-11 (KJV)
[225] Rom. 16:17-18 (KJV)

follow in an attempt to attract more people. They grow in size, people still go out of tradition, then over time the people generally figure out there is no point in attending church and they drop out and the church eventually dies. If your goal is self-pleasure and entertainment, you can live the life you want to live, skip the Compromised Church, make your best life now, save a few hours of time and money. Just use secular motivational speakers. You can't truly live your best life now by attending silly Compromised Churches and throwing your hard-earned money at them; only the preachers cashing those tithe checks will be able to do that.

"In a day when all absolutes are under attack and being destroyed in the hearts and mind of this present generation, there is a tremendous need to maintain sound doctrine, that 'faith which was once delivered to the saints.'"[226] Doctrine must be sound, pure, scripturally based, and most importantly followed. What Hollywood is doing does not produce good doctrine. Many churches have actual doctrinal statements on a website somewhere; they are just not followed. Sound doctrine stands against the false doctrines entering the church. "The Word produced the Church. The Word is not subject to the authority of the fallible church, but the church is subject to the infallible authority of the Word."[227]

The Westminster Confession (1.2) says Scripture is to be interpreted in light of its own purpose and is "Given by the inspiration of God to be the rule of faith and life," and that Scripture interprets itself. (Westminster Confession, 1.9)[228] These creeds and confessions are rooted in concrete historical examples, are intended to be a guide for the proper interpretations of scripture for preaching and witness, are a form of worship unto themselves, and are intended for instruction for Christians, as a manual for education. The great creeds and confessions of the church will clarify and defend Christian truth against attacks, heresy, and

---

[226] Conner, Kevin J. *The Foundations of Christian Doctrine*. Portland, Or., 1980, foreword.
[227] Ibid., 38.
[228] Guthrie, Shirley C. *Christian Doctrine*. Louisville, KY: Westminster John Knox Press, 2018, **12**.

perversions from both within and outside of the church. "The most dangerous heretics the creeds have had to fight are not the openly godless, immoral people who attack the church and the Christian faith from the outside. They are the people within the church . . . who are enthusiastically in favor of the Bible, religion, morality, and the church—but use them to lend authority and respectability to ideologies and methods they consciously or unconsciously want to enthrone in place of God in Christ."[229] But these doctrines and declarations have their place, The Westminster Confession of Faith tells us: "Confessions and declarations are subordinate standards in the church, subject to the authority of Jesus Christ, the Word of God, as the Scriptures bear witness to him . . . Obedience to Jesus Christ alone identifies the one universal church and supplies the continuity of its tradition."[230]

Sin is not the bad part of the Bible, it is the good part. You have to remember "Heaven is for Sinners and Hell is for good people."[231] Sinners that have acknowledged that they have sinned, repented, find their way to heaven by the grace of God. Good people that see themselves as good with no need for a savior, find themselves eternally separated from the Creator that they spent their whole lives rejecting, essentially getting what they want. In repentance we find freedom. By surrendering we find strength. In repentance we find forgiveness. Jesus was a friend to sinners; look at who he associated with. He associated with the bad people, the outcasts of the day. Jesus told the tax collectors and prostitutes, modern-day IRS agents and hookers, that they were going to heaven before the Pharisees and Saducces, which would be referring to some of the elders, deacons, and pastors of the Compromised Churches of today. The religious people. Today we have church people that go to church, get involved in programs, talk religious code, possibly a leader or Pastor, but

---

[229] Ibid., 23.
[230] Guthrie, Shirley C. *Christian Doctrine*. Louisville, KY: Westminster John Knox Press, 2018, **27**.
[231] Ibid., 396.

need to repent, not necessarily for their salvation which they may or may not have, but of sin, which we all have, and return to the Creator. God has no interest in religious activities done for self-promotion. The Bible says that when you do them so that you can receive attention, "You have received your reward in full." The point of mentioning sin is not condemnation, but for freedom. That which puts us in bondage can be shed to find our deliverance.

In High School I took the wrong path. A passionate teenager, I loved fighting, had a passion for rebellion and trouble, and a thirst for hard drinking. I would like to blame following the wrong crowd, but I was the wrong crowd. Suspended so many times, I was finally informally expelled. I ended up conditionally receiving my diploma based on a promise to stay 500 feet away from the school and because I was about to be shipped off to Lackland Air Force Base to begin basic training. I knew I was a bad person because the other bad people told me so. I knew I had sin in my life because sin and rejection and rebellion from God was my life. I embraced Agnosticism and opened the dark doors of Atheism, but even then I lacked the faith needed for that cause. But it was the weight of this sin, the heaviness of the burden, the acknowledgement of all of the wrong that I did that drove me to repentance. It was nothing theologically fancy, just a simple acknowledgement of sin and asking for forgiveness. I was then shipped off to Texas a few days later to begin basic training. Basic training helped get rid of the old life. I was now a military man. But there were scars, bondages, and deep-rooted sins that didn't just magically go away. Some left immediately, others would hang on, linger, always present, bondages that I didn't learn how to fight and overcome until later in life. I struggled through the faith for a while, forgiven, but at the same time carrying the weight of the past with me.

Later in life I would use prayer, fasting, and meditating on the scriptures to free me from these bondages one by one. God does set his people free. But at the time, I was battling to stay in the faith, battling to remember to occasionally read the Bible, battling to free myself from my bondages. The weight of the past, the sins, the bondages of agnosticism sometimes felt like too much. I was still God's sheep, just heavily wounded and scarred. In the depth of the struggles, our Pastor announced that he would no longer follow traditional Christianity but would follow the Seeker Sensitive movement. Me and my wife joined people that left the church as the church split. We instinctively wanted to find a healthy church to go to. My wife found a little church and was told they would see the power of God and evangelize the world. That talk was just for her; it was a little prosperity church that had cult-like characteristics. A cult sounds scary, but this was not a Hollywood cult where you drink poison and chant, but probably similar to your church if you go to a Compromised Church, where the leader paints himself as a religious man but really uses power, manipulation, fear, and control to get his way and sets up his own rules and ideas above God's ways and ideas. My wife got sucked away into the church. I attended occasionally and liked some aspects, they had nice snacks, always a fan for cheese and crackers, but someone who was not meant to conform could never really fit into this kind of structure.

One day I had a possible real estate deal in Florida that I proposed we head to for the winter to escape the Michigan cold. My wife hated the cold, but said she had to ask the Pastor for his permission to go. I angrily scoffed at the Pastor and his entire church. If my wife did not want to go to Florida, we could stay in the frozen tundra of Michigan and try to survive in that habitat, but that would be our decision, not his. The Pastor heard the blasphemy that I had just spoken, and the judgment came down swift and severe. I was labeled toxic and dangerous from the words that I spoke. We already had a fractured marriage, and the pastor was able to use that for his advantage. My wife left me and took our only son. She was not to have contact with me, her parents, siblings, or former friends. Fortunately, after my wife was out of money to give the Pastor, he didn't want anything to do with her anymore. I cried out to God again, this time not for salvation, but for help, not to save me for my eternal soul, but to save me from myself. I found freedom in God and direction from the Bible, not through the church's skits and small groups. Our marriage was restored through the power of God and submitting to his will, not submitting to the will of the pastor.

Some basic declarations of faith over Christian History usually contain items such as the Bible is our authority, the trinity, Man's fall, regeneration, salvation, justification, and sanctification. There are essential doctrinal statements that have been established through Christianity. We have the Deity of Christ, Salvation by Grace, His atoning death and Resurrection, the authority of the Gospel, and the belief in one God. Essential doctrines cover that the Bible is the infallible word of God: Jesus Christ died on the cross as an atonement for our sins, people are saved through the gospel, etc. When prosperity churches are saying that Christ died on the cross for your financial gain, or compromised/seeker churches completely leave out the gospel message or tinker with God's word, they are attacking essential Christian doctrine.

Then there are of course non-essential doctrines. Things that are interesting to reflect on but people can have opposing views on. Calvinism vs Armeniasim is one. Various Bible versions. Church denominations. Dispensationalism and Cessationism. Dispensationalists see the Bible divided into time periods and study the Bible according to that mindset, stages of God's self-revelation. Cessationists believe things like speaking in tongues, healing, and prophecy ceased. There are different ideas on water baptism. Revelations brings us a whole bunch of theories to argue about such as Premillennial, Postmillennial, Covenantal, New Covenant Theology, Dispensational Premillennial, and more. The point is that all of these minor doctrinal differences are something to intellectually explore, but not to create divisions over. We are all one as the body of Christ. Now of course you can't take this too far. If your church is heading towards this progressive view that Jesus was a nice guy or a prophet like Mohammad and God is love and loves everyone and all the religions are really one faith in some kind of New Age progressive march to Heaven, that is not Christianity. It is of the world. The Bible tells us to be in the world but not of it.

The point of theology, doctrine, creeds, and teaching is so that you have a correct understanding of the Bible. For many, an incorrect theology or understanding of God will allow you to retain your salvation, but lead to unnecessary struggles through life. For others, it could cost them their salvation. We have to meet God's requirements, not man's requirements that may tell you to be a moral person or religious person. In order to correctly understand theology, you have to correctly understand the Bible. Otherwise, people will pick a verse or two and base their theology on that. Many Christians fought and risked their lives to fight the evil institution of slavery in 19th-century America, others used the verse "Servants, be subject to your masters with all fear; not only to the good and gentle, but also to the froward"[232] as justification for the movement. When the first World War started, there was not a lot of enthusiasm for another European war, Americans were against it. So some pastors were paid to preach pro-war rhetoric, to justify American involvement in another European War. "A time of war, and a time of peace,"[233] was used as justification for the movement.

Today, one arm of the church twists the atonement to cover financial gain, while the other arm has redefined Christianity completely, eliminating the atonement so we can focus on our lives right now. Together, they have given us the Compromised Church. **Not only does the**

---

[232] 1 Pet. 2:18 (KJV)
[233] Ecc. 3:8b (KJV)

Compromised Church attack reason, logic, and common sense, it also attacks Christian History, Theology, and Doctrine. Christian History, Theology, and Doctrine is not something new, but has been in place for a few thousand years. Constitutions, Creeds, covenants, and statements have been established. We have a framework of ideas, thoughts, and theologies. For 2,000 years, Christian Doctrines, Creeds, Statements of Beliefs, Essential beliefs, have generally marched in the same direction, while encountering many assaults against the faith. While there may have been different wordings, there have been 2,000 years of history, doctrine, theology, creeds, statements, and declarations that point to truth, point to concrete statements, point to the cross. There have always been discourse and divisions, then people would go back to the faith to cement their beliefs. Today, they are being changed, for new purposes and new platforms. The greatest assault against the faith today is being done in house in many areas. Today's Compromised Churches have no theology to follow, doctrine is dictated by Hollywood, and beliefs change as feelings and the mood changes. Entertainment, great speeches, drawing crowds and collecting money is the new doctrine. The theology of the modern Compromised Church is no longer the Study of God, but the study of Man's wants, desires, goals, and happiness.

IX. A Quick Tour In Apologetics

In years past, America was primarily a Christian nation. Secularists and Atheists would put the burden of proof on Christians, to "prove" that Christianity was real. And things were explored, such as apologetics, archaeology, scientific evaluations, moral codes, etc. Piles of evidence would be brought to the table, but there was never one piece of evidence to "prove" Christianity. There is no smoking gun or irrefutable piece of evidence. Now the tables are turned and we are told that there is no God. Scientific theories are brought to the table. Many of the greatest scientific minds of our day have come to the table to try to prove that God does not exist. But while media, public schools, and the entertainment industry indoctrinate our children and many adults with this theory, do they actually have evidence there is no God?

    Science has given us brilliant people such as Einstein, Newton, and Hubble and helped us explore things we didn't even know existed, such as protons, neutrons, cells, and DNA. Scientific developments have led to all sorts of technological advancements and the furtherment of mankind. And Science provides us with concrete, observable, verifiable, and recordable results. Get out two test tubes, put chemicals in each, and see what you come up with. Science has also given us theories, ideas, and hypotheses. There is nothing wrong with theories, testing things, and hypotheses; Edison had 1,000 attempts on his lightbulb, because that is how you learn things. The problem is creating theories and hypotheses and labeling them as facts, before all of the evidence is in.

Theories and hypotheses have been proven wrong in the past. In the 19th century, people were obsessed about the North Pole. They claimed that beyond the Arctic Ice rings, warm currents pushed in to create an open arctic sea, undiscovered lands, and possibly even a tropical paradise. So members of the USS Jeannette launched an expedition and attempted to push through these rings. They never did find a tropical paradise, mostly just a bunch of ice and starvation as they lost their main ship and struggled across the arctic facing hypothermia and frozen limbs along with death and near-death experiences. The survivors were able to find a few neat Woolly Mammoth tusks lying around for souvenirs.[234] We have claims that are made about the projection of asteroids that are supposed to run into the Earth and certainly wipe out the Earth, then end up missing the Earth by a hundred thousand miles. Chonosuke Okamura, a Japanese paleontologist, became convinced that patterns of water seepage in rocks were "mini-fossils" and that life was descended from mini-horses, mini-cows, and mini-dragons. Science gives us neat chemicals, then later finds out that they can't remove some of them from water supplies, like MTBE.[235] When 2020 arrived, Glacier National Park was forced to remove all of its signs stating the park's glaciers would be gone by 2020.[236] You can pick up old high school science books and notice the dates of the age of the Earth have shifted by hundreds of millions of years, prior to the scientific community settling on 4.54 as a good date to use for conformity. So Science has given us pure, concrete, observable results, that have led to wonderful discoveries, along with theories,

---

[234] Sides, Hampton. *In the Kingdom of Ice: the Grand and Terrible Polar Voyage of the USS Jeannette*. United States: Doubleday, 2014.
[235] Newman, Judith. "20 Of the Greatest Blunders in Science in the Last 20 Years." Discover Magazine. Discover Magazine, January 3, 2020. https://www.discovermagazine.com/the-sciences/20-of-the-greatest-blunders-in-science-in-the-last-20-years.
[236] "Glacier National Park Removing All 'Glaciers Will Be Gone by 2020' Signs." Disrn. Accessed March 3, 2020. https://disrn.com/news/glacier-national-park-removing-all-glaciers-will-be-gone-by-2020-signs.

hypotheses and ideas, some of which have led to great discoveries, others of which have been proven wrong.

The age of the Earth gets pushed very hard by science. It seems as if the more time that they give things, the higher probability that there is to make things work. Rocks in Canada and New Zealand get labeled as a few billion years old, so assumptions are made that the Earth is older than that, and these rocks are used as a foundational measuring stick for other items. But what if the dating on the rocks is wrong? Are we doing scientific guesswork at that point? Are dating methods scientific fact or hypothesis? Recorded history goes back 4,000 years or so; this is significantly before that. In one case, a bone fragment was taken in and determined to be millions of years old. Later on, that bone was found to be from someone's dog. Radiometric dating has failed us before. Mount Ngauruhoe located on the north island of New Zealand had samples taken from active lava flows from 1949-1975. They were sent to a respected lab and dated from 0.27-3.5 million years old. A rock sample from the Mount St. Helens 1986 lava flow was dated using Potassium-Argon dating and dated at 0.5-2.8 million years old.[237] Radiometric dating from the volcanic eruption on Mt. Etna in Sicily happened in 122 BC but was radiometric dated to 170,000 - 330,000 years old. The Hualalai basalt eruption happened in Hawaii between 1800-1801 and was dated to 1.32-1.76 million years old. Another Hawaii eruption, the Kilauea Iki basalt, happened in 1959, and was dated to 1.7-15.3 mIllion years old.[238]

But whether you stick by James Usher's date of 4004 BC and see a young Earth or you like the 4.54 Billion number, problems still arise when you figure out how you get the complexity of the universe without a Creator. And an old Earth may pose as many problems for evolution as a young Earth. Scientists claim that the earth would need to spend a lot of

---

[237] Ham, Ken. *The New Answers-Book 1: over 25 Questions on Creation, Evolution and the Bible*. Green Forest, AR: Master Books, 2006, **118**.
[238] Ham, Ken. *The New Answers Book 2*. Green Forest, AR: Master Books, 2008, **52**.

time cooling down after its creation, leaving some 400 million years for evolution to take place. Then you are left dealing with issues such as how to form an amino acid. You need the right bonds between them, you have right-handed and left-handed ones, and they have to link up in the correct sequence. "Run the odds of these things falling into place on their own and you find that the probability of forming a rather short functional protein at random would be one chance in a hundred thousand trillion trillion trillion trillion trillion trillion trillion trillion trillion. That's a ten with 125 zeroes after it!"[239] And this just gets you one very basic protein molecule. To get a cell you could need 500 of these protein molecules. Amino acids randomly interacting for hundreds of trillions of years are not going to magically create life. "To suggest chance against those odds is really to invoke a naturalistic miracle. It's a confession of ignorance. It's another way of saying, 'We Don't know."[240] Chandra Wickramasinghe observed: "The emergence of life from a primordial soup on the Earth is merely an article of faith that scientists are finding difficult to shed. There is no experimental evidence to support this at the present time. Indeed all attempts to create life from non-life, starting from Pasteur, have been unsuccessful." Microbiologist Michael Denton stated "The complexity of the simplest known type of cell is so great that it is impossible to accept that such an object could have been thrown together suddenly by some kind of freakish, vastly improbable event. Such an occurrence would be indistinguishable from a miracle."[241]

Things do evolve and change over time, we have all kinds of new species and varieties. God created original kinds and modern species descended from this. Humans did some of this and Nature has also. Orchardists have crossed a plum and apricot to make a plumcot. Horses

---

[239] Strobel, Lee. *The Case for a Creator: a Journalist Investigates Scientific Evidence That Points toward God*. Grand Rapids, MI: Zondervan, 2004, **229.**
[240] Ibid., 229-230.
[241] Geisler, Norman L., and Frank Turek. *I Don't Have Enough Faith to Be an Atheist*. Wheaton, IL: Crossway Books, 2007, 121.

and donkeys have been bred to make mules. The finches in the Galapagos islands have different beak sizes. Various breeding techniques have given us new types of dogs. Mice and bedbugs are evolving to become more resistant to pesticides and poison. Hawaii has numerous species, endemic to, or only found in Hawaii. Things do evolve on their own. It is called microevolution; we see a lot of it, and we see it before our eyes. But there are limitations to this. Dinosaurs did not turn into birds, and monkeys did not turn into men. Pond slime did not rise up to form humans. Over the millions of years that this supposedly would have taken place, there would be hundreds of millions or hundreds of trillions of transitional fossils. Transitional fossils would be fossils showing dinosaurs evolving into birds or monkeys turning into man. Transitional fossils, or the "missing link," are still missing. This is not due to lack of effort or lack of imagination.

The Piltdown Chicken supposedly showed us the missing link on how birds evolved from dinosaurs. National Geographic prominently published their "proof" of evolution and prominently displayed the skeleton, and it was quickly picked up by the global media. The fossil was allegedly smuggled from China showing a dinosaur with birdlike plumage. But after getting global attention, it was found to be a hoax, as the tail of a dinosaur and the body of a bird were fused together, so it was quietly dismissed.[242] There have been more attempts to find the missing link, or transitional fossils, between man and monkey. We have Piltdown Man, discovered in the Piltdown quarries of England. This was proof of man's evolution from primate, until it was found out that the skull was human and the jaw was from an orangutan whose teeth had been filed to crudely resemble the human wear pattern.

We have Cro Magnon Man and Neanderthal man. These were originally considered human by scientists and then downgraded to that of

---

[242] Austin, Steven A. "Archaeoraptor: Feathered Dinosaur from National Geographic Doesn't Fly." The Institute for Creation Research. Accessed February 13, 2020. https://www.icr.org/article/archaeoraptor-feathered-dinosaur-from-national-geo.

an apelike creature. The Neanderthal man has a low forehead, long narrow skull, protruding upper jaw, and are deep-chested, large-boned individuals with a strong build. Neanderthals were human in every respect. The cranium capacity, which relates to brain size, is actually larger than modern man. It appears that the missing link here is that some skeletons show rickets or arthritis. We have the Nebraska man, pushed by the media as the missing link; entire displays were created and numerous pictures published replicating this man with his entire family, but it was later found that a single pig tooth and a human skull were used for the creation of Nebraska Man. We have Java Man in which a tooth, skullcap, and thigh bone was used to push a transitional fossil piece. Using these methods, you can take a tooth, skullcap, and thigh bone from your grandfather to recreate that he was the Incredible Hulk. And then we have Lucy, which supposedly shows an erect transitional link between the monkey and human. The pose Lucy is presented in leads to the feel of a transitional piece, but that is just creativity in how the skeletal system is put on display. These types of apes are knuckle walkers and have ape-like hands and wrists; it takes imagination, creative staging, and a manipulative pose to pull this off.

We have a few experiments that have been used as evidence for evolution. They get taught in schools around the country and are still found in some high school and college textbooks. For instance, there's 1953 Miller-Urey experiment in which some of the chemical building blocks of life were created by sending an electric spark through a mixture of gases which were supposed to simulate the Earth's primitive atmosphere. Some simple organic compounds were created, and it was presented as how life originated. But the problem in this experiment was that they had to make an assumption on Earth's early atmosphere. This early atmosphere would not have contained any oxygen. If oxygen was present, the experiment would have literally been blown up. Most scientists today reject this theory, but it is still being used as an example. Chemist Robert Shapiro, especially critical of the Miller-Urey experiment, said that we have reached a situation "Where a theory has been accepted as fact by some, and possible contrary evidence is shunted aside." This is "Mythology rather than science."[243]

We have Darwin's tree of life which shows the branching pattern that would result from this process and shows how species are related through evolutionary history. Pictures of Darwin's tree of life litter high school and college textbooks. But this is problematic, as our fossil records show all of the fossils arriving on the scene during what scientists call the Cambrian explosion; all of the major animal groups arrive at once, right at the start. Almost as if they were created or something, contradicting the major theme of Darwin's theory. We have the pictures of ape men that line the science book which are drawn from imagination, from missing transitional fossils that do not exist. Darwin predicted that numerous intermediate fossils would be discovered in the future, but they have not been discovered. Transitional fossils need to be absorbed with a lot of faith. One problem with the transitional fossil idea is that many transitional forms would not likely survive. If Iguanas started sprouting feathers, they are less likely to be able to survive, not more likely. Colin Patterson, senior paleontologist at the British Museum of Natural History, housing the world's largest fossil collection of 60 million specimens, confessed: "If I knew of any [evolutionary transitions], fossil or living, I would certainly have included them [in my book *Evolution*]."[244]

Haeckel's embryos still get pushed in textbooks. These pictures show early vertebrate embryos that were drawn from various classes of vertebrates to show they are virtually identical in the earlier stages. This

---

[243] Wells, Jonathan. *Icons of Evolution: Science or Myth?: Why Much of What We Teach about Evolution Is Wrong*. Washington: Regnery, 2002, 27.
[244] Hanegraaff, Hank. *Christianity in Crisis: the 21st Century*. Place of publication not identified: Thomas Nelson, 2009, 330.

created powerful proof for Darwin's theory. Yet these are faked drawings. The early stages were faked, the drawings were doctored a bit, deliberately distorted to fit his theory. This was exposed in the 1860s, yet many people still remember the drawings from their childhood. Stephen Jay Gould noted that Haeckel "Exaggerated the similarities by idealizations and omissions" and concluded the drawings have "Inaccuracies and outright falsification."[245]

But while the educational institutions and media thrive on pushing theories, there is dissent within the scientific community. According to Larry Hatfield in Science Digest, "Scientists who utterly reject evolution may be one of our fastest growing controversial minorities. . . Many of the scientists supporting this position hold impressive credentials in science."[246] They issued a defiant statement: "We are skeptical of claims for the ability of random mutation and natural selection to account for the complexity of life." "Careful examination of the evidence for Darwinian theory should be encouraged."[247] German Researcher Klaus Dose wrote in 1988 that "Current theory is a scheme of ignorance. Without fundamentally new insights in evolutionary processes. . . this ignorance is likely to persist."[248]

John Horgan, a leading science journalist, conceded that scientists have no idea how the universe was created or "How inanimate matter on our little planet coalesced into living creatures. . . Science, you might say, has discovered that our existence is infinitely improbable, and hence a miracle."[249] Nobel Prize winner Francis Crick stated: "An honest man, armed with all the knowledge available to us now, could only state that in

---

[245] Wells, Jonathan. *Icons of Evolution: Science or Myth?: Why Much of What We Teach about Evolution Is Wrong*. Washington: Regnery, 2002, **93-94**.
[246] Strobel, Lee. *The Case for a Creator: a Journalist Investigates Scientific Evidence That Points toward God*. Grand Rapids, MI: Zondervan, 2004, **31**.
[247] Ibid., 32.
[248] Wells, Jonathan. *Icons of Evolution: Science or Myth?: Why Much of What We Teach about Evolution Is Wrong*. Washington: Regnery, 2002, **24**.
[249] Strobel, Lee. *The Case for a Creator: a Journalist Investigates Scientific Evidence That Points toward God*. Grand Rapids, MI: Zondervan, 2004, **42**.

some sense, the origin of life appears at the moment to be almost a miracle, so many are the conditions which would have had to have been satisfied to get it going."[250] Biochemist Klaus Dose's 30 years of research revealed: "A better perception of the immensity of the problem of the origin of life on Earth rather than to its solution. At present all discussions on principal theories and experiments in the field either end in stalemate or in a confession of ignorance."[251] Francis Crick laments, "Every time I write a paper on the origin of life, I swear I will never write another one, because there is too much speculation running after too few facts."[252] The original event itself, The Big Bang, is recorded as, "A supernatural event that cannot be explained with the realm of physics as we know it."[253] Sir Fred Hoyle stated: "A commonsense interpretation of the facts suggests that a superintellect has monkeyed with physics, as well as chemistry and biology, and that there are no blind forces worth speaking about in nature."[254]

Charles Darwin started questioning his idea of natural selection in the fifth edition of *On the Origin of Species*, and this was close to finalized by the sixth edition. Darwin stated: "To suppose that the eye with all its inimitable contrivances for adjusting the focus to different amounts of light, and for the correction of spherical and chromatic aberration, could have been formed by natural selection, seems, I freely confess, absurd in the highest degree."[255] We have to remember that while doctrinational institutions push monkey-to-man evolution as fact, Darwin just had it as a theory. When the Duke of Argyll stated to Darwin that "It was impossible to look at the numerous purposeful contrivances in nature and not see

---

[250] Ibid., 42.
[251] Geisler, Norman L., and Frank Turek. *I Don't Have Enough Faith to Be an Atheist*. Wheaton, IL: Crossway Books, 2007, **121**.
[252] Ibid., **121**.
[253] Strobel, Lee. *The Case for a Creator: a Journalist Investigates Scientific Evidence That Points toward God*. Grand Rapids, MI: Zondervan, 2004, **70**.
[254] Ibid., 78.
[255] Hedtke, Randall. *Secrets of the Sixth Edition: Darwin Discredits His Own Theory*. Green Forest, AR: Master Books, 2010, **58**.

that intelligence was their cause," Darwin "Looked at [him] very hard and said, 'Well, that often comes over me with overwhelming force; but at other times,' and he shook his head vaguely, adding, 'It seems to go away.'"[256]

Monkey teeth will continue to be filed down to represent humans, and bones will be bleached, and stories will be created. Facts will be twisted and fables will be spun. If faith is meant to be questioned and explored, so can scientific hypotheses. But we do have the answer: "In the beginning God created the heavens and the Earth."[257] Get away from the TV and the city, head into nature, and you will find: "The heavens declare the glory of God; And the firmament shows His handiwork."[258] His fingerprints are all over his creation. The complexity of creation is before us and it is meant to be discovered, explored, and felt. "For the invisible things of him from the creation of the world are clearly seen."[259]

The Bible is the infallible Word of God, the best-selling book of all time with over 50 billion copies distributed, and the bedrock of our faith. According to Wycliffe Global Alliance, a portion of scripture has been translated in over 3350 of the 7099 existing languages. It has provided a source of strength and comfort and changed lives across the globe. The Bible is the most popular book in World History. "About 30 years ago, for the British and Foreign Bible Society to meet its demands, it had to publish "One copy every three seconds day and night; 22 copies every minute day and night; 1369 copies every hour day and night; 32,876 copies every day in the year."[260]

The Bible itself attests to the authorship of the Almighty. "**Long ago, at many times and in many ways, God spoke to our fathers by the**

---

[256] Ibid., 141.
[257] Gen. 1:1 (NIV)
[258] Ps. 19:1 (NKJV)
[259] Rom. 1:20 (KJV)
[260] McDowell, Josh. *Evidence Demands a Verdict*. Arrowhead Springs, San Bernardino: Campus Crusade for Christ International, 1972, 18.

prophets."²⁶¹ The New Testament scholar, FF Bruce wrote convincingly, "The Bible is not simply an anthology; there is a unity which binds the whole together." The uniformity can be seen throughout the book, pointing to the cross, pointing to the Creator, and pointing to truth. 40 different authors over a 1500-year span written in 3 different languages in different times and places, and it does not contradict itself. It is not just that the Bible claims itself as divine over 3,000 times; the Bible itself validates it. While it is continually attacked on all fronts, continually challenged, the validity always shines through. Jesus frequently read and quoted the Bible, which of course was the Old Testament at the time. "And he said unto them, These *are* the words which I spake unto you, while I was yet with you, that all things must be fulfilled, which were written in the law of Moses, and *in* the prophets, and *in* the Psalms, concerning me."²⁶² "All scripture *is* given by inspiration of God, and *is* profitable for doctrine, for reproof, for correction, for instruction in righteousness."²⁶³

The accuracy of the scribes writing the Bible has been questioned by scoffers, then the Dead Sea Scrolls came out and scholars were amazed at how accurate the Biblical translations were. This should not be surprising as this was the life's work of many of the scribes. The historical accuracy of the Bible has been questioned, then new revelations would come out confirming the historical accuracy of the Bible. The secular historical sources that we have through antiquity and through the time of Christ confirm the validity of the Bible. The Historical accuracy of the New Testament is confirmed through sources such as: Josephus, Suetonius, Eusebius, Philo, Clement, Tertullian, and Hegesippus, contemporary non Biblical writers that confirm the Biblical accounts. The Old Testament is also confirmed with historical sources from antiquity

---

[261] Heb. 1:1 (ESV)
[262] Luke 24:44 (KJV)
[263] 2 Tim. 3:16 (KJV)

but also archaeology. Nelson Glueck, the prominent archaeologist stated: "In all of my archaeological investigations I have never found one artifact of antiquity that contradicts any statement of the Word of God."[264] There have been Numerous Archaeological explorations that have confirmed the validity of the Bible. Abraham's home city of Ur was excavated, Solomonic cities found in 1 Kings such as Hazor, Megiddo, and Gezer have been excavated. Sargon's palace as mentioned in Isaiah 20, has been discovered after critics originally questioned the existence of this Assyrian king. Critics questioned the story of Belshazzar in the Bible, then Nineveh is excavated and Belshazzar's palace is discovered. Biblical kings such as David, Omri, Ahab, Jehu, Joash, Jeroboam II, Uzziah, Menahem, Ahaz, Pekah, Hoshea, Hezekiah, Manasseh and Jehoiachin have all been found. Archaeological discoveries have unearthed many Biblical civilizations such as the: Hittites, Egyptians, Caananites, Assyrians, Babylonians, Persians, Moabites, Philistines, Edomites, Ammonites, and Syrians.[265] Archaeology has cleared up many historical dates and confirmed Biblical reliability.

The Bible gets attacked on multiple fronts, but when you are willing to take the time to research the questions, you will find logical answers. The gospels are questioned for containing different stories and accounts of the life of Jesus. But of course they are going to contain different stories, because you have four different accounts from four different perspectives, but not one sentence directly contradicts another sentence. The story of the sun standing still in the book of Joshua gets attacked because the sun always stands still; the Earth would have stopped its rotation. But to these Israelite soldier farmers that were fighting in a life-and-death battle that day, the sun did exactly that: it stood still to allow them to finish the battle. God answered the heart of the prayer, not the correct scientific logistics of it. And the one that created the laws of

---

[264] McDowell, Josh. *Evidence Demands a Verdict*. Arrowhead Springs, San Bernardino: Campus Crusade for Christ International, 1972,22.
[265] Eames, Christopher. "So Much Archaeological Proof!" theTrumpet.com. Accessed February 13, 2020. https://www.thetrumpet.com/18639-so-much-archaeological-proof.

nature can miraculously, temporarily set aside the laws of nature. Numerous Biblical prophecies are powerful, so some Historians have tried to post date prophecies, or push the dates forward by hundreds of years to render the prophecy pointless. Then other evidence through History or Archaeology will come around to prove the correct Historical date, showing the power of the prophecy.

The New Testament in the Bible contains numerous prophecies, some fulfilled, some concerning the end times and partially fulfilled or yet to be fulfilled. There are numerous fulfilled prophecies just dealing with the birth of Christ. Including that he was born of a virgin, the son of God, the seed of Abraham, coming from the Davidic line, born at Bethlehem, presented with gifts, that he shall be a prophet, judge, and priest. The King will enter Jerusalem on a donkey, be resurrected, betrayed for silver, mocked, smitten, and spit upon, crucified with thieves, hated without cause, bones not broken, and buried in a rich man's tomb. The Old Testament has numerous prophecies dealing with Palestine, Tyre, Moab and Ammon, Edom, Sidon, Samaria, Gaza and Ashkelon, Jericho, Petra, Nineveh, and Babylon. By looking at just eleven Old Testament prophecies, the probability of these eleven prophecies coming true, if written in human wisdom, is 1 in 5.76×10^{59}.[266] The Creation of Israel in 1948 is a modern-day miracle along with Israel fighting 100 million Arab invaders in 1967 & 1973. Isaiah 44:28 mentions Cyrus by name saying that he will build Jerusalem and God's temple. This is a weird prophecy as it was already built. But then Nebuchadnezzar destroys it in 586BC, and 160 years later, Cyrus takes control and does exactly that.

One interesting Old Testament prophecy has to do with the city Tyre. Ezekial 26:3-4 tells us: "Therefore thus says the Lord God, 'Behold, I am against you, O Tyre, and I will bring up many nations against you, as the sea brings up its waves. They will destroy the walls of Tyre and break

---

[266] McDowell, Josh. *Evidence Demands a Verdict*. Arrowhead Springs, San Bernardino: Campus Crusade for Christ International, 1972, **319**.

down her towers; and I will scrape her debris from her and make her a bare rock."[267] God is against the city of Tyre and said it would bring many nations against her. So the empire of Babylon comes against Tyre and destroys the entire mainland in 585 BC. Then the Persian Empire takes off from where Babylon left off and controls this area, keeping it to a pile of rubble. But between these two great empires, the prophecy was never really completely fulfilled, as the debris was never scraped as bare as a rock. Plus some of the inhabitants survived the attacks and fled the mainland and lived on an island near the mainland, creating a powerful island city. But then a few hundred years later, Alexander the Great rose his Greek Empire from the tiny city state of Macedonia to create the newest world empire and defeat Persia. When Alexander saw this island of Tyre it infuriated him, but he had no real way to attack, as he had primarily a land-based army at the time. So in 332, Alexander started taking the remnants, debris, and rubble of the ancient land-based portion of the city of Tyre and throwing it into the Ocean. The debris made new land, and he started creating his own land bridge or causeway out to the island city of Tyre. By the time he reached the island of Tyre, he scraped all of the debris from the original city of Tyre: "I will scrape her debris from her and make her a bare rock." Alexander then eliminated the island city; it is now a place the fisherman can go to dry out their nets. "It shall be a place for the spreading of nets in the midst of the sea."[268]

Jesus was once asked what the greatest of his commandments was. They were expecting something from the Ten Commandments: do not lie, do not steal, do not commit adultery, or one of the other ones. But Jesus replied: "Thou shalt love the Lord thy God with all thy heart, and with all thy soul, and with all thy mind, and with all thy strength: this *is* the first commandment. And the second is like, *namely* this, Thou shalt love thy neighbour as thyself. There is none other commandment greater than

---

[267] Ezek. 26: 3-4 (NASB)
[268] Ezek. 26: 5 (KJV)

these."[269] While this can oftentimes get overlooked, loving God with your mind is listed as one part of the greatest commandment. Search the scriptures as the Bereans did, they did it daily. If you are Christian and go to a potentially Compromised Church, don't take whatever the leadership says as truth; assume deception, and use the Bible as your authority and truth. A good or great Pastor will not mind being held to Biblical authority. While there is no need to cause contention over minor doctrinal differences, staying silent in the midst of evil is embracing evil. For those who are Agnostic, go ahead and examine Atheism, examine your questions, find answers, just like you did when you started questioning the faith. Staying in the dark is ignorance. Search for the truth. The Bible tells us faith is a gift, but like all gifts or lack thereof, things can be developed. Study the Bible, apologetic books, leave parts of your past behind, find answers for your questions, they are all there, even if you are filled with them. Pray, search for truth, and love God with all of your mind. This is an act of worship. Theodore Roosevelt was born with a weak chest and breathing conditions, hours of exercise developed him into a barrel-chested man and leader of our country. Ben Carson was born in the poor city of Detroit, unlikely to ever hold a significant job; his mom drove him to libraries to read books, and he became one of the greatest brain surgeons to ever live. Those labeled with learning disabilities have gone on to achieve academic excellence. Likewise, those who currently have weak faith can diligently strengthen their faith and end up alongside the great people of faith such as Abel, Enoch, Noah, Abraham, Sara, Moses, and Rahab.

> Here is a man who was born in an obscure village, the child of a peasant woman. He grew up in another village. He worked in a carpenter shop until He was thirty. Then for three years He was an itinerant preacher.

---

[269] Mark 12:30 (KJV)

He never owned a home. He never wrote a book. He never held an office. He never had a family. He never went to college. He never put His foot inside a big city. He never traveled two hundred miles from the place He was born. He never did one of the things that usually accompany greatness. He had no credentials but Himself . . .

While still a young man, the tide of popular opinion turned against him. His friends ran away. One of them denied Him. He was turned over to His enemies. He went through the mockery of a trial. He was nailed upon a cross between two thieves. While He was dying His executioners gambled for the only piece of property He had on earth—His coat. When He was dead, He was laid in a borrowed grave through the pity of a friend.

Nineteen long centuries have come and gone, and today He is a centerpiece of the human race and leader of the column of progress.

I am far within the mark when I say that all the armies that ever marched, all the navies that were ever built; all the parliaments that ever sat and all the kings that ever reigned, put together, have not affected the life of man upon this earth as powerfully as has that one solitary life.[270]

He never wrote a book, and yet all the libraries of the country could not hold the books that have been written about Him. He never wrote a song and yet He has furnished the theme for more than all the songwriters combined. He never founded a college, but all the schools put together cannot boast of having as many students. He never practiced medicine, and yet He has healed more broken hearts than all the doctors far and near.[271]

---

[270] This essay was adapted from a sermon by Dr James Allan Francis in "The Real Jesus and Other Sermons" © 1926 by the Judson Press of Philadelphia (pp 123-124 titled "Arise Sir Knight!").
[271] McDowell, Josh. *Evidence Demands a Verdict*. Arrowhead Springs, San Bernardino: Campus Crusade for Christ International, 1972, 135.

X. The Revitalized Church

Slight deception will precede the great deception. While the great deceiver may not be upon us yet, deceivers have made a marriage with the church; at this point they are a fabric of the church. There have always been cults and deception, but now deception is interwoven into some of the mainstream churches. Eschatological events can be tricky; various groups and cults have been predicting the end of the world for some time now. But the Bible makes it clear that we will not know an exact date, as it will come as a "Thief in the night"[272] and "But about that day or hour no one knows, not even the angels in heaven."[273] This kind of would have been a deal killer for the various cult members that killed themselves because their leader said the world was ending the next day. Maybe they should have read the book for themselves. While no one knows the exact date, you can watch the signs. It is getting closer.

Numerous prophetical events have already come to pass. Some things are yet to come. False teachers will deceive and ensnare many. We are told about wars, earthquakes, pestilences, and famines. Many scholars think the Bible points to a digital cashless monetary system, using "The Mark," and a one-world government. This has partly come into play with the European Union uniting and global open borders. Israel is going to be

---

[272] 1 Thess. 5:2b (YLT)
[273] Matt. 24:36 (KJV)

a key player in Eschatological events as it always has. Its own miraculous conception in 1948 and the 7-day war was the start of things to come. We are told: "That there shall come in the last days scoffers, walking after their own lusts."[274] And before the end comes there will be "A falling away"[275] of those of the faith. We are also told: "For there shall arise false Christs, and false prophets, and shall shew great signs and wonders; insomuch that, if it were possible, they shall deceive the very elect."[276]

One of the largest signs left is going to be the global one-world religion. The exclusivity of the Christ claim poses a problem for Christianity. Christianity makes a claim that Christ died on the cross for the salvation of your sin, and by not believing in this, you will be eternally separated from God. This cannot conform with other religions. True Christianity, the version preached by Christ and his followers, does not conform. Fortunately, the compromised new version of Christianity will allow the Buddhists, Muslims, Atheists, and Hindus, to get together, sing some songs, love one another, and be a better you. The exclusivity of the cross claim will not be love, but Orwellian hate speech that will push true Christianity away from the new globally socially accepted Christianity. True Christians will be persecuted and others will conform. There will be one leader to control the world with another leader to control this new religion. He will be referred to as the Antichrist, but make no mistake, there has already been many terrible men that have been Antichrist to God's plan such as Antiochus, Diocletian, and Nero, and there may be more prior to "The" Antichrist setting his stage.

This paper was not written to or about one particular church, but many. I have had the opportunity to travel, visit, and live in various spots across America, from Kona to the Carolinas, from Fairbanks to Florida. I have met many beautiful pastors and people doing incredible things

---

[274] 2 Pet. 3:3b (KJV)
[275] 2 Thess. 2:3 (KJV)
[276] Matt. 24:24 (KJV)

across America with strong healthy churches powerfully impacting the community. A healthy, doctrinally sound church is a beautiful thing, filled with vibrant and powerful believers. I have also seen Compromised Churches focusing on their own destruction, or that of their sheep. And then there are many good men with good hearts that are getting deceived. Pastors caught in their own bondages, that need to put up a good front, but in some cases, it is the blind leading the blind. I have seen Churches that have embraced the word of God then get caught in legalism, and then churches that neglect the word of God and get trapped in sin and bondages. Churches that are striving for the Almighty and churches that aren't as concerned. Churches focused on building God's kingdom and others focused on their own kingdom as they battle amongst themselves for congregants, church size, and social status. Churches that preach a unification theme that all religions lead to the same God, and others that preach on the blood of Jesus. Self-seeking churches and outwardly focused gospel churches.

A line has been drawn in the sand. Some may not want the line, but regardless it has been placed. To get past the line, two paths are presented. One path claims to bring safety, ease, and comfort as it seeks to align itself with the world and avoid what is to come. The other path chases after the heart of God, has a foundation, has a direction; it may present some challenges, but it is the path that leads to the Glory of God. While two paths are presented, only one path can be taken, and this will become more clear as time passes. Many American churches need a directional change that will cry out to God and seek after the heart of God, that can use the gifts given to it to bring in thousands of new people. Not to create a more impressive church or build legacies and egos but to save souls and change lives across America. That churches will hold hands as they lead a new movement across the country that will not make the world comfortable and seek to hold its hand but will terrify it as hearts and lives are transformed for the glory of God. A movement that will relegate this verse to a prophecy in the future and not a modern-day event: "For the time will come when they will not endure sound doctrine; but after their own lusts shall they heap to themselves teachers, having itching ears; And they shall turn away their ears from the truth, and shall be turned unto fables."[277]

For years the church would impact the culture, today the culture impacts the church. Bach and Michelangelo are now replaced by structured messages designed so people feel comfortable. As the church tries to fit in and blend with the world, its true purpose is getting lost. Becoming accepted precedes spreading the message. Friendship evangelism replaces intentional evangelism. As Christians and churches cower in fear of being mocked by the world, the message gets hidden. Mega churches rise up in glitz, glamour, and congregational size and attract thousands to deliver messages to itching ears. Sound doctrine is replaced by feel-good doctrine. Self-empowerment, fuzzy messages, compromises, plays, and entertainment precedes spreading the gospel and pursuing a life of righteousness. As each church battles each other and tries to build its own kingdom, instead of Christ's kingdom, the true purpose gets lost. Moral relativism and avoidance of absolute truth are becoming the mantra of the modern-day church. The line is blurred between right and wrong, justice and injustice, righteousness and unrighteousness. Without a source for absolute truth, anything goes as we slide down the slippery slope to apostasy. Everything is all relative as everyone can live out their own convictions. The Trinity, abortion, the deity of Christ, the Virgin Birth, Attonement, the Resurrection, everything can be reinterpreted based on self-needs. Without an absolute standard, what is now forbidden will become embraced, as we continue our slide away from a foundation, away from God.

---

[277] 2 Tim. 4:3 (KJV)

While the prosperity gospel is one deceptive arm that is leading thousands away from the throne of Christ to propped-up Americanized idols, other churches now have a Carnegized gospel that shows us how to win friends, influence people, and be a better moral person. Meeting felt needs, psychological training, and life skills success takes precedence over living a life of righteousness devoted to following Christ. The definition of success in America is a prestigious job and a large paycheck. Should the definition of success in the church be measured by the same standards? Do we value congregational size and good performances or changed lives and strong doctrine? Should growing large churches just for the sake of growing large churches be the ultimate goal? "Growth for the sake of growth is the ideology of the cancer cell."[278] An argument can be made whether or not the self-help, variety-seeker, motivated preachers are using their intellect and influence to gradually wean Christians away from the gospel and God. But what cannot be argued is that a copy of a copy gradually loses its power and luster. Why follow a copy when you can follow after and chase the heart of God directly and have a relationship with our Father in heaven? He needs to be our Father, he needs to be our source, and he needs to be our guidance.

In America, most people strive for success and focus on entertainment. Bringing some parts of this into the church is not necessarily bad, and can even be a good thing. A big successful church focused on God and not itself can change lives, the community, and the Nation. What is bad is compromising on the primary message, which is the cross. Powerful speakers, digital displays, nice buildings, and marketing materials are not the problem. They can help. The problem is when you take out the message and all you are left with is powerful speakers, digital displays, nice buildings, and marketing materials. It may wow and awe, impress and excite, bring recognition and attention, but

---

[278] Quote attributed to Edward Abbey

that unto itself cannot save and change lives. Imagine taking your girlfriend to the finest 5-star steakhouse in town. It is a beautiful restaurant in the nicest part of town. The table is set with a fine tablecloth, and there is a beautiful bouquet of flowers on the table. The table is even set with a bunch of forks and spoons of different sizes and shapes that you don't know what to do with. Your server is funny, courteous, witty, and keeps your beverages topped off. The appetizers are some of the finest appetizers you have ever had, and the salad is a meal unto itself. But when it is time for the main course, the steak, the waiter announces that they are all out of steaks. You don't go to a steakhouse and not be able to get a steak, you don't go to a golf course without golf balls, you don't go to a pool without water, but apparently you can go to church and not get the gospel.

"What is truth?" It is the question Pilate posed to Jesus. It is the question posed by numerous souls throughout history. It is the question that has scattered people and sent some searching and wandering. Buddhists have searched Nirvana for truth. Humanists have searched reason for truth. Philosophers have searched for truth in wisdom, Hippies have searched for it in love, and materialists have searched for it in possessions. Fortunately for Christianity, the foundation for truth has already been established. There is a bedrock, a foundation for the faith. This is found in the Bible. The Bible and Jesus Christ is the foundation on which the faith has been built. Every evangelical movement built on this has produced long-lasting fruit. Movements built on man's methods produce short term temporary growth that later leads to dead and rotten fruit, a sandy foundation.

Pilate gets blamed a lot for the crucifixion of Christ. But If you reread the story you can tell that Pilate really did not want to crucify Jesus and just went along with the pressure and the demands of the people. He said "I find in him no fault at all."[279] Pilate's wife wanted to let Jesus go due to a dream that she had, and Pilate seemed content in just doing that. Pilate even tried to release Jesus to the people, but the people overwhelmingly voted to have Barabbas released. "Pilate therefore went forth again, and saith unto them, Behold, I bring him forth to you, that ye may know that I find no fault in him."[280] Later on in the story, he reiterates: "I find no fault in him."[281] Then, when they wanted to crucify Jesus "because he made himself the Son of God,"[282] Pilate heard that and "He was the more afraid."[283] At this point, Pilate is filled with stress, fear, and anxiety; he wants to relax his inner convictions and listen to his wife. This Jesus guy was thrust upon him, and he wants nothing to do with his death. Pilate then tries to negotiate with Jesus and try to find some type of loophole on how to release him. After talking with Jesus, the scripture says "Pilate sought to release him."[284] His conscience is burdened, and he does not want this man's blood on his hands. But the crowd tells him: "If you release this man, you are not Caesar's friend."[285] He is forced to face the ultimate peer pressure and possible career killer. Pilate relents and presents Christ to the Jews saying "Behold your King!"[286] The reply of course was "We have no king but Caesar."[287]

    Pilate had no desire to crucify Jesus, he wanted to set him free, he was just not strong enough to stand up against the popular opinion of the day, and so he would not make that stand. Pilate seemed to be a decent governor of Judea; he even built a nice aqueduct system for the Jewish

---

[279] John 18:38b (KJV)
[280] John 19:4 (KJV)
[281] John 19:6b (KJV)
[282] John 19:7b (KJV)
[283] John 19:8b (KJV)
[284] John 19:12A (KJV)
[285] John 19:12B (ESV)
[286] John 19:14b (KJV)
[287] John 19:15b (KJV)

people[288] to give them fresh water.[289] He could even be considered a nice guy compared to other Roman leaders like Nero or Diocletian. Nevertheless, the blood is on his hands, and he will account for the murder he authorized. Today, churches are filled with elders, deacons, pastors, and laymen that deep down inside know or have seen that their church is filled with wrong doctrine, lies, deception, and is running away from God's truth. They might make a comment or two, might make a few efforts for change, but ultimately they settle down behind their leader and stay with the opinion of the people. It may be due to money, comfort, cowardness, or their social status in the religious community. While they might make light resistance or put in a subtle effort as Pilate did, ultimately they do nothing. Make no mistake, the blood of the sheep getting slaughtered is on your hands as it was on Pilate's.

Whatever these seeker, attractional, entertainment, purpose-driven churches once were, hanging on to a remnant of God, they are no more. The original compromise has shifted to such an extent in the next generation, many churches have completely removed the Biblical foundation, the gospel, and the truth. Compromised Churches are feeding our next generation. When the National Study of Youth and Religion took a look at adolescents' faith, they found they believe that the central goal of life is "To be happy and to feel good about oneself."[290] Christ has been removed from out of the messages, hearts, lives, signs, and buildings across America. Crosses are being removed from many churches in America. But new purposes are created, tithes are collected, enthusiasm mustered, motivational speakers paid, as each empire tries to build its own kingdom. Original Christianity, the version practiced by millions over

---

[288] The Jewish people never really appreciated the nice fresh water aqueduct system Pilate built for them. Maybe they were ungrateful. Or maybe it was because PIlate built it over a cemetery, making the water impure for them to drink. Also because he took the money to finance this project from the Jewish Temple.
[289] Wroe, Ann. *Pontius Pilate*. New York: Modern Library, 2001, 106.
[290] "Moralistic Therapeutic Deism--the New American Religion." The Christian Post. Accessed March 5, 2020. https://www.christianpost.com/news/moralistic-therapeutic-deism-the-new-american-religion.html.

decades, was about building God's kingdom for the glory of God. Today it is about building man's kingdom, man's legacies, and man's institutions. Make no mistake, while you are out dropping your checks in buckets, waving cars to the parking lot, recruiting people to your social club, you are not doing God any favors, but just promoting your own social status in the church, building legacies, and providing paychecks. You will receive affirmation from leadership, recognition, acceptance, and social status. But, "They have received their reward in full."[291]

Today Christianity is a vast battlefield. The world attacks on all angles, continually mocking, lying, and casting doubt from the media, Hollywood, and the educational system. Those that don't fight, conform, compromise, and get indoctrinated. Charles Spurgeon stated: "To be a Christian is to be a warrior. The good soldier of Jesus Christ must not expect to find ease in this world: it is a battlefield. Neither must he reckon upon the friendship of the world; for that would be enmity against God. His occupation is war."[292] Yet when we enter some of our churches, instead of getting Biblical training, apologetics, passionate fighting for the faith, we get entertainment, doubt, and compromise. Nothing is creating a stronger generation of unbelievers in America right now than the faithful caught in compromised institutions. God is not impressed that you managed to sneak off the coach on an occasional Sunday to grace him with your presence by sauntering in to watch a play and eat a doughnut at the local self-help church. Time would have been more efficiently utilized sleeping in or watching the football game. Acts 20:29: "I know that after my departure fierce wolves will come in among you, not sparing the flock; and from among your own selves will arise men speaking twisted things, to draw away the disciples after them. Therefore be alert, remembering

---

[291] **Matt. 6:2b (KJV)**
[292] Spurgeon, Charles H, Sermon No. 2201, "The Sword of the Spirit." in *The Complete Works of C.H. Spurgeon, Vol 37*. Delmarva Publications, USA.

that for three years I did not cease night or day to admonish every one with tears."

Amongst the wreckage of the battlefields lies the Compromised Churches. Slaughtered sheep and wounded lamb crawling in circles stumbling in their search for truth. But as water is withheld to the parched desert traveler, truth is withheld from the lambs that need it. You might be able to stumble around a Compromised Church and find a basketball court, roller coaster, theater, playground, brothel, or bar, but you will seldom find any truth, reason, or substance. Compromised Churches mostly exist to soothe souls and make people feel better about how they spend their Sunday mornings and feel like a good person. But atheists can stay home and not go to church and many of them are also good people. I am not sure that God gets any satisfaction that Johnny begrudgingly dragged himself off the coach Sunday morning to saunter into church to nap in the back row and nurse off his hangover. Might as well stay home, save some gas, and help the environment a bit. In reality, the church is delivering what some of the people want, so there should be no cause for alarm. However, mixed amongst those wanting ears itched, are struggling souls looking for truth, salvation, and redemption for their lives. This is why it is devastating. "It is a solemn thing, and no small scandal in the kingdom, to see God's children starving while actually seated at the Father's table."[293]

The Bible gives us clear commands on not judging people outside of the church or even judging each other in regards to sin and salvation. "Judge not, that you be not judged."[294] But truth in the church needs to be examined. The Bereans "searched the scriptures daily"[295] to see if what was being said was true. Paul's letter to the Corinthian church commands us to judge the church: "What business is it of mine to judge those outside

---

[293] Tozer, A. W. *Pursuit of God*. Abbotsford, WI: Aneko Press, 2015.
[294] Matt. 7:1 (ESV)
[295] Acts 17:11b (KJV)

the church? Are you not to judge those inside?"[296] "The correction of false doctrine in the New Testament is always a public matter, and never a private one."[297] Paul publicly rebuked Peter,[298] Hymenaeus, Alexander,[299] and Alexander the coppersmith.[300]

All of Paul's letters to the churches warn about false teaching and give orders for fighting it. It was a primary concern for him, and it should be for us today. Paul was especially concerned for Timothy and Titus. Timothy was told to stay in Ephesus "So that you may command certain men not to teach false doctrines any longer."[301] Paul tells Timothy: "The Spirit clearly says that in later times some will abandon the faith and follow deceiving spirits and things taught by demons. Such teachings come through hypocritical liars, whose consciences have been seared as with a hot iron."[302] Timothy was commanded to boldly teach the truth of God's Word[303] and recognize error and point it out to the brethren.[304] Things did not go well for Hymanaeus and Alexander who were "Handed over to Satan."[305] "If anyone teaches a different doctrine and does not agree with the sound words of our Lord Jesus Christ and the teaching that accords with godliness, he is puffed up with conceit and understands nothing. He has an unhealthy craving for controversy and for quarrels about words, which produce envy, dissension, slander, evil suspicions, and constant friction among people who are depraved in mind and deprived of the truth, imagining that godliness is a means of gain."[306] Paul tells Timothy that these false teachers are: "Evil men and impostors."[307]

---

[296] 1 Corinthians 5:12 (NIV)
[297] McConnell, D. R. *A Different Gospel*. Peabody, MA: Hendrickson Publishers, 1995, 88.
[298] Gal. 2:14
[299] 1 Tim. 1:20
[300] 2 Tim. 4:14
[301] 1 Timothy 1:3-7 (NIV)
[302] 1 Timothy 4:1-2 (NIV)
[303] 1 Timothy 4:11
[304] 1 Timothy 4:6
[305] 1 Tim. 1:20
[306] 1 Tim. 6:3-5 (ESV)
[307] 2 Tim. 3:13 (ESV)

And to: "Rebuke them sharply, so that they may be sound in the faith and will pay no attention to Jewish myths or to the commands of those who reject the truth."[308] In regards to the truth, we are given instructions to guard it.[309] Jesus himself was not very happy with the state of the church either. He told us to: "Beware of false prophets, which come to you in sheep's clothing, but inwardly they are ravening wolves."[310] He consistently mocked two influential religious sects of the day, the Pharisees and Sadducees. When Jesus did visit the church and saw people selling things, he started flipping tables over and referred to the church as a "Den of thieves."[311]

It is the job of each Christian to search, examine, and fight for truth in the church, as the Bereans did. The church is not supposed to be established as a Theocracy, with one man wielding spiritual control over his congregation. Christ is the head of the church. All Christians can have a direct relationship with God and search the scriptures for truth. "Seek and ye shall find; knock, and it shall be opened unto you."[312]

Many times, Compromised Churches can deliver great inspirational speeches, put on good performances, inspire faith, create hope, bring a smile, or create enthusiasm. Many give to various charities that do make great contributions to the Kingdom of God. On occasion, there can be some good that comes out of it. Likewise, a congregant can get healed from a Benny Him crusade, or someone's financial outlook can increase after throwing some money at Kenneth Copeland. The law of probability relates marginal probabilities to conditional probabilities. These things are going to happen, just not in the abundance that they should. Likewise, someone can visit Las Vegas and see good performances, create hope, feel love or bring a smile. Someone's financial situation can certainly change if

---

[308] Titus 1:13-14 (NIV)
[309] 2 Tim. 1:13-14
[310] Matt. 7: 15 (KJV)
[311] Mark 11:15-17
[312] Matt. 7:7b (KJV)

they strike luck on a slot machine, with or without a four-leaf clover, and if coming from a winter climate, the change in weather could clear them of a cold. They might even reach the depths of their depravity in a Vegas brothel, acknowledge they are a sinner that needs God, and cry out to him.

This does not limit the possibility that God could actually physically heal someone at a healing crusade. There are many crusades, the name of Jesus is used, so genuine healings can happen. Likewise, a random person can pray for someone and they can be healed; there is no special anointing from the man on stage. A broken system can still produce results just as a failing business can still produce revenue. I met an interesting atheistic individual that believed in some type of spiritualism. He starts his day by chanting money, money, money to increase his financial situation. I asked "How is that going for you" and he responded "Good, I found a quarter the other day on the side of the road." So it may be working out just fine for him. But the widow is losing what she has left, the business person is draining his capital, and the single mom is losing her ability to provide for her children by not turning to God, but turning to the man on the TV. Broken systems can produce results, just not as effective as a well-functioning system, such as turning to God himself. As the Israelites flocked to their false Gods instead of the true God, today people flock to false preachers looking for cures instead of the true God.

There is a vast field with rolling hills. At one end of the field, there is a light that comes down on the field. Sheep are grazing in this section of the field, they are safe and secure, there is peace. But there are not many sheep here. The sheep are wandering away from the light, heading in the opposite direction, away from the safety and security. Some are at the edge of the field ensnared in the thickets, the thorns piercing their skin. Some wander in circles in the middle of the field, confused, wounded, and hurt. Blood drips from them; it stands as a stark contrast against their white fur. Others seem determined to head in the opposite direction of the light, towards the dark woods where the wolves abound. Some even have a hard time moving, because their wounds are so deep, their gashes are so vast, the cuts are so plentiful that they are making an attempt to head to the light, to safety, but it is as if they do not have enough strength. "Today, if you hear his voice, do not harden your hearts as in the rebellion."[313]

> Luke 15:11-32: And he said, A certain man had two sons: And the younger of them said to his father, Father, give me the portion of goods that falleth to me. And he divided unto them his living. And not many days after the younger son gathered all together, and took his journey into a far country, and there wasted his substance with riotous living. And when he had spent all, there arose a mighty famine in that land; and he began to be in want. And he went and joined himself to a citizen of that country; and he sent him into his fields to feed swine. And he would fain have filled his belly with the husks that the swine did eat: and no man gave unto him. And when he came to himself, he said, How many hired servants of my father's have bread enough and to spare, and I perish with hunger! I will arise and go to my father, and will say unto him, Father, I have sinned against heaven, and before thee, And am no more worthy to be called thy son: make me as one of thy hired servants. And he arose, and came to his father. But when he was yet a great way off, his father saw him, and had compassion, and ran, and fell on his neck, and kissed him. And the son said unto him, Father, I have sinned against heaven, and in thy sight, and am no more worthy to be called thy son.
>
> But the father said to his servants, Bring forth the best robe, and put it on him; and put a ring on his hand, and shoes on his feet: And bring hither the fatted calf, and kill it; and let us eat, and be merry: For this my son was dead, and is alive again; he was lost, and is found. And they began to be merry. Now his elder son was in the field: and as he came and drew nigh to

---

[313] Heb. 3:15 (ESV)

the house, he heard musick and dancing. And he called one of the servants, and asked what these things meant. And he said unto him, Thy brother is come; and thy father hath killed the fatted calf, because he hath received him safe and sound. And he was angry, and would not go in: therefore came his father out, and intreated him. And he answering said to his father, Lo, these many years do I serve thee, neither transgressed I at any time thy commandment: and yet thou never gavest me a kid, that I might make merry with my friends: But as soon as this thy son was come, which hath devoured thy living with harlots, thou hast killed for him the fatted calf. And he said unto him, Son, thou art ever with me, and all that I have is thine. It was meet that we should make merry, and be glad: for this thy brother was dead, and is alive again; and was lost, and is found.[314]

Today, there are waves of true Christians and pastors that have wandered away from Christ for whatever reason. They once knew God, once tasted his goodness, but are currently heading in another direction, maybe because they were deceived, or maybe because they lost interest in following God for another reason. Maybe a pain or infliction caused a turning away or hardening of the heart. God is calling them back, God is calling you back. It is time to return. It is time to pull people out of the institutions and toward the heart of God.

There is an Alaskan preacher named Jimmy Stewart. He was a faithful and well-spoken Baptist preacher for many years. Alaska shows some of the most beautiful aspects of God's creation. Waterfalls lead to more waterfalls which lead to rivers. Whoever originally called this place Seward's folly never visited in the summertime. So Jimmy was up in this remote Alaskan cabin, and the propane lights started flickering. He went down in the crawl space to check the problem. What he didn't fully realize at the time was the heavy feeling of the air as he was moving through this crawlspace, as the air was filled with dense propane gas. A slight spark

---

[314] Luke 15: 11-32 (KJV)

ignited the propane and sent Jimmy flying and incinerated his skin. His son managed to pull what was left of Jimmy out of the crawlspace and airlifted him to the hospital. Jimmy, the ET technicians, and his son knew that the remnants of Jimmy really weren't going to the hospital but to the cemetery. The seasoned ER technician knew that men in half as bad condition did not survive these types of things. But Jimmy didn't waste his dying thoughts and breath on why God would allow something like this to happen to his faithful preacher. He used it to witness to the ER technician who was trying to keep Jimmy alive for a few minutes longer. The gospel message that the ER technician received from what was left of this man "Shook him to the core."

What would happen to Christianity if the preachers of today, the preachers of some of the churches, quit preaching self-help messages of empowerment, or twisted scriptures around for financial gain, and preached the gospel. Or if they quit focusing just on themselves, their ministry, their legacy, and focused on the sheep and the lost. What would happen to America if the Christians today focused more on the gospel message and less on the self-improvement seminars found in the churches. What would happen to Christianity if the people in churches actually cared about people outside of the institutions they are building. Fortunately there are a few of them still around today. Jimmy is actually still one of them; he somehow managed to survive. I heard him preach a sermon at a church in Hawaii. He honestly wasn't much to look at. I hate to say it, but plastic surgery can apparently only do so much; this guy isn't going to be put on the cover of GQ magazine anytime soon. But the message that he gave, the true message of Christ crucified and the Cross of Christ, trusting in God through any circumstance, shook everyone in that room to the core.

The prosperity church has abandoned the almighty to bow their knee to the almighty dollar. The seeker churches have morphed into giant tax free entertainment meccas that self-help you on your way to success. Together they have given us the Compromised Church, a church not built on the word of God, but on the compromises of the world. A church that does not strive for righteousness, but strives to fit in. A church that does not aim for the Glory of God, but for the glory of man. But the church has gone through dark times before and has come through. "Upon this rock I will build my church; and the gates of hell shall not prevail against it."[315] Today we have righteous pastors that are ready to step up and lead an army of people towards the glory of God. We have Godly people that are ready to take on more challenges. But we also have people, churches, and Pastors that have made mistakes, have taken the wrong road, but are ready to repent, and ready to change. After all, that is what the gospel message is all about. And God has been waiting for you. It is time. Sola Scriptura, Sola fide, Sola gratia, Solus Christus, Soli Deo gloria.

---

[315] Matt. 16:18 (KJV)

Appendix

The Ten Solutions

1. Reject the Seeker / Attractional church model

What started under the seeker church model has morphed into something new and now has given us many names: The Attractional church, Entertainment church, Universalistic church, Emergent church movement, New Age movement, or Moralistic Therapeutic Deism.[316] They all mean one thing:, if it is a church without the basic gospel message, it is a Compromised Church. Nowhere in Christian History has the central theme of Christianity been hidden to attract converts. There have been no effective Christian campaigns that hid the gospel message, in order to advance the gospel message. The message was never removed, to proclaim the message. You can't go to a steakhouse and not get a steak, you can't go to a golf course and not find a golf ball, you don't go to the pool without water, but apparently you can go to church and not find the gospel.

---

[316] "Moralistic Therapeutic Deism--the New American Religion." The Christian Post. Accessed March 11, 2020. https://www.christianpost.com/news/moralistic-therapeutic-deism-the-new-american-religion.html.

"It is treason to men's souls to conceal the plain truth of salvation beneath a cloud of words: where God's honour and man's eternal destiny are concerned, everything should be as clear as the sun at noonday."[317] Sometimes it is not even hidden beneath clouds of words, but rather just completely eliminated. The same message that caused scores of Christians to be torn apart and tortured as waves of blood fed the Earth, is the same message that is now hidden by the church. What was once silenced by torture, starvation, and execution, is now being voluntarily silenced for legacies, money, and building sizes. The message that Paul used to compose the New Testament, that God sacrificed his son for, that Augustine wrote about, Luther saved the church with, Whitefield and Wesley started a Great Awakening with, Spurgeon saved countless souls with, is now a message that is hidden below convenience.

2. Reject and renounce the prosperity gospel

While your church might not necessarily preach this gospel, it is infiltrating congregants' hearts, minds, and actions. It is on TV and in the books they read. The idea that you can purchase favor, anointing, and blessings from God by giving money to the man on TV is the same works-based financial system that Luther fought against. You cannot purchase favor from God through the charlatan on the TV set as a peasant couldn't buy his salvation through indulgences from the Pope in 15th-century Europe. God sent his son Jesus out of love for the entire world. It is a free gift, received upon repentance. Paying money to the man on TV to receive this free gift makes as much sense as writing a personal check directly to

---

[317] MacArthur, John. *Ashamed of the Gospel: When the Church Becomes like the World*. Wheaton, IL: Crossway Books, 2010, 277-278.

Jeff Bezos to mail you some packages. Amazon already delivers free packages; you don't need to write a second check to Bezos to get them, just as Christ already covered your atonement on the Cross, you don't need to cut a check to Copeland.

Some pastors don't preach the prosperity gospel. Yet they wink and turn a blind eye while their sheep allow their minds to be filled with these ideas. Silence can be construed as an endorsement, it *is* an endorsement. In dysfunctional families, one parent may be an abusive alcoholic, the other may be quiet and do nothing. Psychologists have created a term for the other parent that watches their own child get abused and does nothing to stop it: an enabler. While they may not do it intentionally, they enable the dysfunction in their household. Some Compromised Churches do not necessarily preach prosperity gospel sermons, yet they hint at it, their sheep are getting consumed by it, so they are enablers. A righteous church would not want to be associated with the prosperity gospel as a good man would not want to be associated with pedophilia; they are both filthy. The prosperity churches have abandoned the almighty, to bow their knee to the almighty dollar. Unfortunately, what some people today are calling Pastors, Prophets, and Teachers, the Bible is calling False Teachers, wolves, and Heretics.

> When we get the abundant life wrong, we get Jesus wrong. When we get faith and confession wrong, we get salvation wrong. Why is that a huge deal? Because all roads that the prosperity gospel paves lead to hell."[318]

> For there shall arise false Christs, and false prophets, and shall shew great signs and wonders; insomuch that, if it were possible, they shall deceive the very elect.[319]

---

[318] Hinn, Costi W. *God, Greed, and the (Prosperity) Gospel: How Truth Overwhelms a Life Built on Lies.* Grand Rapids, MI: Zondervan, 2019, **100.**
[319] **Matt. 24:24 (KJV)**

3. Add substance to the Church

"Simple obedience to the Word of God is being ignored, as the church has become more a place of human interest rather than the place to pursue the Kingdom of God."[320] People today are overwhelmed with work, families, and responsibilities. While technological advances have made many tasks easier, in many cases, the technology designed to free us has made many slaves to the system. People are taking a break from their busy weeks to get substance. Coffee, donuts, jokes, plays, smiles, and an entertaining sermon are not going to cut it. They need substance, they need the gospel, they need truth. In a world that attacks from every angle, Educational systems, Hollywood, the culture, reading a few verses from the Bible on a weekly basis is not going to cut it. Get the sheep infused with the Bible, get the members into apologetics training, provide substance, provide truth. Substance does not scare people off, rather It changes lives and provides direction to those who need it.

> It is a solemn thing, and no small scandal in the kingdom, to see God's children starving while actually seated at the Father's table ... They minister constantly to believers who feel within their breasts a longing which their teaching simply does not satisfy."[321]

> Many U.S. churches today have "forgotten" their purpose, becoming entertainment-driven social organizations eager to blend in with secular culture instead of focusing on biblical discipleship."[322]

---

[320] Covarrubias, Loren. *Why is the Devil in My Garden?* Call from the Mountain Media, 2011, 122.
[321] Tozer, A. W. *Pursuit of God*. Abbotsford, WI: Aneko Press, 2015, x.
[322] "David Jeremiah Warns Modern Church Is Entertainment-Driven Social Organization Afraid of Controversy." The Christian Post. Accessed February 10, 2020.
http://www.christianpost.com/books/david-jeremiah-warns-modern-church-is-entertainment-driven-social-organization-afraid-of-controversy.html.

4. Change the non Evangelization policy of the church

The idea behind the seeker movement was to hide the gospel on Sundays and provide in-depth Biblical training on Wednesdays. But somehow the idea of hiding the gospel didn't get limited to just Sundays, it became part of the fabric of the movement. The idea of protecting the seekers by keeping them away from the danger of the gospel permeated through the congregation. But it is this message that the people really needed, and the Bible commands to spread. The book of Matthew concludes with this command, commonly known as the Great Commission: "Go therefore and make disciples of all the nations, baptizing them in the name of the Father and of the Son and of the Holy Spirit, teaching them to observe all things that I have commanded you; and lo, I am with you always, even to the end of the age. Amen."[323] While all of the gospels retell the same story from each of their own firsthand accounts and perspectives, they all include the great commission. Mark tells it like this at the end of his account: "Go into all the world and preach the gospel to every creature. He who believes and is baptized will be saved; but he who does not believe will be condemned."[324] The gospel message is not a secret to be held with shame, but rather a declaration of love designed to be spread.

> And every day, in the temple and from house to house, they did not cease teaching and preaching that the Christ is Jesus."[325]

> And Paul dwelt two whole years in his own hired house, and received all that came in unto him, Preaching the kingdom of God, and teaching those things which concern the Lord Jesus Christ, with all confidence, no man forbidding him."[326]

---

[323] Matthew 28:19-20 (NKJV)
[324] Mark 16:15-16 (NKJV)
[325] Acts 5:42 (ESV)
[326] Acts 28: 30-31 (KJV)

5. Eliminate control, let go, and Create a new Legacy

Control has weaved itself into the framework of some churches. When a leader's words take precedence over the Word of God, it is problematic. Christ is supposed to be the head of the church, not man. "And he is the head of the body, the church: who is the beginning, the firstborn from the dead; that in all things he might have the preeminence."[327] "Christ is the head of the church: and he is the saviour of the body."[328] While this can be troublesome in an American society built on accomplishments and legacies, a church is not built on religious accomplishments, no matter how great they are, or about creating an institution onto yourself, but based on God's will and chasing after the heart of God. "And upon this rock I will build my church; and the gates of hell shall not prevail against it."[329] Legacies are not about what we accomplish on Earth, or religious accomplishments, but about following the will of God and working towards the Glory of God.

6. Follow God's Word, not the Culture

George Orwell, in his novel 1984, coined the term "doublethink," which referred to the ability to hold two completely contradictory beliefs in one's mind simultaneously, while accepting both of them at the same time. Today, churches cite the word of God, yet preach doublethink. It is one or the other. Infuse your church with the Bible and the teachings of God or follow the culture and do what they say, it is one or the other. The

---

[327] 1 Col. 1:18 (KJV)
[328] Eph. 5:23b (KJV)
[329] Matt. 16:18b (KJV)

culture may attack Christianity from multiple directions, but the Church needs to stand strong against it. Church policy and sermons should not be structured from Hollywood, yet structured from the Word of God.

> Do not be conformed to this world, but be transformed by the renewal of your mind, that by testing you may discern what is the will of God, what is good and acceptable and perfect."[330]
>
> Do not love the world or the things in the world. If anyone loves the world, the love of the Father is not in him. For all that is in the world—the desires of the flesh and the desires of the eyes and pride in possessions—is not from the Father but is from the world. And the world is passing away along with its desires, but whoever does the will of God abides forever."[331]

7. Eliminate Lies and Deception

Adolf Hitler starved the Jewish children in his concentration camps and referred to it as a "Low-calorie diet." Lying is listed as one of the main things the Lord hates, and deception is his friend. Lying was singled out to be included as one of the Ten Commandments. And "The Lord detests lying lips."[332] The Compromised Church is built on lies and deception. Scripture is twisted around to fit the agenda instead of creating an agenda based on scripture. When the reality of the faith is one thing, and you present an image of Christianity that is another thing, you are involved in deception and probably incorporating lies to maintain this deception. As the used car salesman smiles and tells the widow that the car with a bad transmission and knock in the engine is a great vehicle and will last her many years, so is the pastor that smiles and tells his people that giving

---

[330] Rom. 12:2 (ESV)
[331] I John 2:15-17 (ESV)
[332] Prov. 12:22 (NIV)

him a few bucks and warming a few seats is all they need for salvation, or that they can purchase favor from God for a few bucks. Snake-oil salesmen are not only found in used car parking lots.

> If anyone is ashamed of me and my words in this adulterous and sinful generation, the Son of Man will be ashamed of them when he comes in his Father's glory with the holy angels."[333]

> Beware of manufacturing a God of your own: a God who is all mercy, but not just; a God who is all love, but not holy; a God who as a heaven for every body, but a hell for none; a God who can allow good and bad to be side by side in time, but will make no distinction between good and broad in eternity. Such a God is an idol of your own, as truly an idol as any snake or crocodile in an Egyptian temple. The hands of your own fancy and sentimentality have made him. He is not the God of the Bible, and beside the God of the Bible there is no God at all.[334]

8. Establish strong doctrine, preach correct theology

Over the course of Christian History, we have been given doctrine, creeds, covenants, declarations, and statements of faith. Truth has been composed into declarative statements. "In a day when all absolutes are under attack and being destroyed in the hearts and mind of this present generation, there is a tremendous need to maintain sound doctrine, the "Faith which was once delivered to the saints"'.[335] Doctrine must be sound, pure, scripturally based, and most importantly followed. What Hollywood is producing does not produce good doctrine.

---

[333] Mark 8:38 (NIV)
[334] J.C. Ryle
[335] Conner, Kevin J. *The Foundations of Christian Doctrine*. Portland, Or., 1980, foreword.

"Blessed is the man that feareth the Lord, that delighteth greatly in his commandments."[336] But whether a church is run by a governing body, or whether it is a non-denominational church, the Bible needs to be the framework and fabric of the Church. The church and Christian faith need to be built upon sound and unchanging doctrinal pillars. "Whosoever transgresseth, and abideth not in the doctrine of Christ, hath not God. He that abideth in the doctrine of Christ, he hath both the Father and the Son. If there come any unto you and bring not this doctrine, receive him not into your house, neither bid him God speed."[337] And: "That we henceforth be no more children, tossed to and fro, and carried about with every wind of doctrine."[338] Over the course of Christian History, we have been given doctrine, creeds, covenants, declarations, and statements of faith. Truth has been put together into declarative statements. We have the Apostles Creed, Nicene Creed, Creed of Chalcedon, The Heidelberg Catechism, Second Helvetic Confession, amongst others. If it is not clear that the Bible is the standard for truth, then you are going to encounter a situation where man's word takes precedence over God's word, and where a leader's opinions can trump the Word of Truth.

Being an independent church or being part of a larger denomination can be a great thing, but the covering needs to be the Holy Spirit, and the doctrine needs to be the Word of God. Churches can not spend time chasing after whatever cultural fads the world is providing. Fads will come and go, yet God's word remains. The Bible needs to be the source for inspiration, not someone else's ideas that may or may not be practical. "Now the Berean Jews were of more noble character than those in Thessalonica, for they received the message with great eagerness and examined the Scriptures every day to see if what Paul said was true."[339]

---

[336] Psalm 112:1b (KJV)
[337] 2 John 9-10 (KJV)
[338] Eph. 4:14 (KJV)
[339] Acts 17:11 (NIV)

9. Insist on Biblically correct versions

There are numerous very accurate Bible versions out there today. While some versions may have gotten to the original better than others, we have a plethora of accurate versions to pick from. The KJV is the original bestseller in recent history and the ESV seems to be taking its place today. Young's Literal Translation is very accurate and underappreciated. The NASB touts itself as the most accurate, while the RSV and NRSV have been standards in many churches. The NIV carries a certain nostalgia for many. Out of this group of versions, some versions may be able to stake a claim that they are a more accurate or better translation than their competitors, and that is fine. What is not fine is to take the liberty to change around the meaning of the words to fit your theories of what God was trying to say, instead of just translating what God actually said.

Some versions have changed the words, to give the Bible a new meaning, or created supplemental readings, to gain greater control over their groups. Jehovah's Witnesses have their New World Translation and Watchtower writings, Mormons use a heavily footnoted Bible and the Book of Mormon. Christian Science has the writings of Mary Baker Eddy, Unitarian Universalists have their secular humanist writings, The New Age Movement has the Aquarian Gospel of Jesus Christ, some Seventh Day Adventists are using the Clear Word Bible, and those of the New Apostolic Reformation have their Passion Translation.

Other groups have distorted things to extreme extents. "The Hitler Bible" would be one example. Communist China's remake with Confusicism embedded in it. Anton Lavey's Satanic Bible is not exactly recommended reading for congregants. But whether a few words are changed around or you change around the entire book, you are still distorting it, you are still putting man's words above God's words. And if the Christian community allows this, radical departures from the truth will be the expectation, rather than the exception. John 8:31 "If you abide in my word, you are truly my disciples."

"So is my word that goes out from my mouth: It will not return to me empty, but will accomplish what I desire and achieve the purpose for which I sent it."[340] When you are paraphrasing God's word to fit your agenda or intentionally or unintentionally paraphrase it to fit your preconceived notions, you are allowing the world to alter the word of God. This started during the Reagan administration, as slight changes were made, and things are changing to a greater extent today. The Bible has always been reinterpreted by people to fit their needs, and now the actual words are being changed to fit their agendas and create what is right in their own minds. In his radio address in response to this, former president Ronald Reagan stated: "It will not dawn on them that it has already been gotten right."

10. Solution

We do not have to guess at how God would run a church because he has already shown us in the Bible. The New Testament church format and formula for growth is clearly outlined throughout the New Testament. Acts and other books detail the rampant growth of the church amidst heavy persecution. It would seem as if the early church was destined to fail, when all of the major participants of the movement were beaten, killed, or exiled. Interestingly enough, that did not happen and the church experienced its most powerful growth during this time period. Other periods of revival in church history were in 1517 when Martin Luther

---

[340] Isaiah 55:11 (NIV)

attacked the Church who also prevented their people from accessing the Bible. The Americas saw powerful revivals in the 20th century led by Jonathan Edwards and George Whitfield. The Old Testament provides countless stories of God's chosen people doing their own thing, heading towards destruction, repenting, then turning back towards God. Israel wanted to continually prop a man up or an idol in place of God, and God would continually call his people back to him. The cycle continues today. The church needs to turn to the heart of God himself, not prop up another man or institution in front of that. A foundation needs to be laid on the Word of God, and not modeled after the latest trends and movements, but after Christ himself.

> Instead of being told how desperately I am in need of God, I am repeatedly told how much God needs me. Instead of being exhorted to pick up my cross and follow Christ, I am told that Jesus wants to be my partner in the plan I have to rid my life of all struggles and challenges.[341]

> The church has always faced the temptation to modify the gospel or make it secondary to a given political, philosophical, or cultural agenda....What is different today is that the message of the cross is being ignored even by those who claim to be saved by its message.[342]

> For the time will come when they will not endure sound doctrine; but after their own lusts shall they heap to themselves teachers, having itching ears; And they shall turn away their ears from the truth, and shall be turned unto fables."[343]

> We can not stay silent as the blade of death runs through God's church.[344]

---

[341] Goggin, Jamin, and Kyle Strobel. *The Way of the Dragon or the Way of the Lamb: Searching for Jesus Path of Power in a Church That Has Abandoned It*. Nashville: Thomas Nelson, 2017, 14.
[342] Lutzer, Erwin W., and Eric Metaxas. *When a Nation Forgets God 7 Lessons We Must Learn from Nazi Germany*. Chicago: Moody Publishers, 2016, **139-140**.
[343] 2 Timothy 4:3-4 (KJV)
[344] Erwin Lutzer

The Seven Churches

Revelations can be considered a bit of a complicated book with different interpretations. However, there seems to be a consensus that the seven churches at the start of the book refer to seven contemporary churches in that time and they also represent all churches in all ages and the state of the church during the end times. The churches mentioned are:

The church in Ephesus – The apostolic church – Ephesus was the religious and commercial center of Asia. They are told: "I know your works, your toil and your patient endurance, and how you cannot bear with those who are evil, but have tested those who call themselves apostles and are not, and found them to be false. I know you are enduring patiently and bearing up for my name's sake, and you have not grown weary. But I have this against you, that you have abandoned the love you had at first."[345] This church was actively engaged in the mission of Christ, fought false teachers, but lost their first love. They are instructed to repent and return to that first love.

Smyrna – The martyr church – They are encouraged to persevere through the tribulation and stay faithful until death, and they will be given

---

[345] Rev. 2:2-5 (ESV)

a "Crown of life." They are materialistically poor but rich in spiritual things. Polycarp amongst others was martyred here, this is the church under tribulation and persecution.

Pergamos: This was a beautiful art-filled city settled along the Caicus river. It was also a center of worship for the pagan gods. This is the church that is settled in the world and dealing with fornication; they made both religious and moral compromises to blend in with the pagan influences that were surrounding them. However, they "Did not deny my faith."[346] And are told: "Repent; or else I will come unto thee quickly and will fight against them with the sword of my mouth."[347]

Thyatira – They are told that "I know your works"[348] and then it lists love, works, service, faith, and patience, seems like a great place. But they allow a false prophetess named Jezebel who would not repent, to roam around and deceive the people and lead them into compromise. This should not have been allowed. "Behold, I will cast her into a bed, and them that commit adultery with her into great tribulation, except they repent of their deeds."[349] But "He that overcometh, and keepeth my works unto the end, to him will I give power over the nations."[350]

Sardis is brought up next. This church is asleep, they are dead, lifeless, and unrepentant. "Remember, then, what you received and heard. Keep it, and repent. If you will not wake up, I will come like a thief, and you will not know at what hour I will come against you."[351] While this church is mostly a lost cause, there are a few people left. "Yet you have

---

[346] Rev 2:13b (ESV)
[347] Rev 2:16 (KJV)
[348] Rev. 2:19a (ESV)
[349] Rev. 2:22 (KJV)
[350] Rev. 2:26 (KJV)
[351] Rev. 3:3 (ESV)

still a few names in Sardis, people who have not soiled their garments, and they will walk with me in white, for they are worthy."[352]

Philadelphia: This is referred to as the church in revival. They are keeping the word of God even though they have little strength; they get no condemnation. "For thou hast a little strength, and hast kept my word, and hast not denied my name."[353]

The church of Laodicea gets the final letter. They are in the final state of apostasy. A wealthy and industrious city, they are rich and believe they need nothing, but are actually wretched, miserable, and poor. Sir William Ramsay calls them "The city of compromise." There is no acclamation here, only condemnation. "I know thy works, that thou art neither cold nor hot: I would thou wert cold or hot. So then because thou art lukewarm, and neither cold nor hot, I will spue thee out of my mouth."[354] Apparently lukewarm water was standard in this city, whether it was icy water from the mountains that became lukewarm by the time it traveled to them or water from the hot springs, that eventually turned lukewarm. The lukewarm state is mentioned three times here. There is hope at the end as it states: "As many as I love, I rebuke and chasten: be zealous therefore, and repent."[355]

---

[352] Rev. 3:4 (ESV)
[353] Rev. 3:8b (KJV)
[354] Rev. 3:15-16 (KJV)
[355] Rev. 3:19b (KJV)

For Additional Information:

Questions, comments, or would like additional information? Were you wounded by the church and need help? Email: equip717@gmail.com

CPSIA information can be obtained
at www.ICGtesting.com
Printed in the USA
BVHW041815130820
586346BV00011B/285